Manuel Miguens, O.F.M.

THE
VIRGIN
BIRTH

An Evaluation of
Scriptural Evidence

Christian Classics, Inc.
205 WILLIS STREET, WESTMINSTER, MD. 21157
1975

Contents

THE VIRGIN BIRTH

INTRODUCTORY REMARKS

Not long ago Raymond E. Brown, S.S., published a paper under the title *The Problem of the Virginal Conception of Jesus*.[1] The paper had been previously delivered in the James Memorial Chapel of Union Theological Seminary, N.Y.C.; and was subsequently printed again, substantially unchanged, as the first of two chapters making up Brown's booklet *The Virginal Conception and Bodily Resurrection of Jesus*.[2] It is to this booklet that the following page numbers refer.

In his short introduction to *The Problem* the author notes that "In Protestantism the question of the virginal conception has been debated for a long time. In some quarters it has been settled with a negative response about historicity" (p. 23). As for Roman Catholicism, Brown feels that "after Vatican II the solid front (on this issue) is cracking in many places" (p. 23). So he decided to undertake a discussion of the problem because "no one has yet discovered a protection against the calumny of oversimplification" (p. 26).

The author points out that his only concern in regard to Mary's virginity is the bodily virginity of Mary as she conceived Jesus. The implication is that he does not consider the way in which Jesus emerged from the womb nor the problem of whether Mary bore other children *after* Jesus. Brown also warns —and this should be carefully noted—that his concern is not primarily theological, it is *historical,* namely: to explore whether the Catholic belief in Jesus' virginal conception by Mary rests on a sound historical basis. Such an analysis is needed—he maintains—because "it cannot be an answer . . . that, since

[1] Published in *TheolStud* 33 (1972) 3–34.
[2] Published by the Paulist-Newman Press, Paramus, N.J., 1973.

1

Christians of the past accepted the virginal conception, we must follow in their footsteps blindly" (p. 30).

The problem, in fact, is whether or not the olden Christian belief is a means to express a merely religious or theological idea, namely, God's direct intervention and particular interest in bringing this man, the Savior, into the world. It is Brown's contention that, "while Matthew and Luke apparently accepted the virginal conception as historical, we cannot be certain where they got their information on this point. . . . Consequently, we must face the possibility that *in good faith* the evangelists have taken over an earlier belief *in virginal conception that does not have an authentic historical basis.* In short, the presence of the virginal conception in the infancy narratives of two Gospels carries *no absolute guarantee of historicity"* (p. 31f; italics mine). It is noted in footnote 37 that "the evangelists were not sophisticated beyond their times."

At the end of his exposition Brown concludes: "My judgment, in conclusion, is that the totality of the scientifically controllable evidence leaves an unresolved problem. . . . Part of the difficulty is that past discussions have often been conducted by people who were interpreting ambiguous evidence to favor positions already taken" (p. 66f).

Very recently Joseph Fitzmyer, S.J., published a paper on the same subject.[3] This paper also had been previously delivered at the Fifth Annual Seminar of the Bishops of the United States, at the Catholic University of America. His point of view is that of Brown, and his reading of the New Testament is the same, with the exception of some details which, however, lead to the same conclusion as that of Brown. Fitzmyer is more emphatic and more explicit when he insists that "a palatable interpretation of the New Testament data" (p. 572ff) would be to consider the presentation of the virginal conception of the New Testament as a theologoumenon, the definition of which is

---

[3] Fitzmyer Joseph A. 'The Virginal Conception of Jesus in the New Testament', *TheolStud* 34 (1973) 541–575.

given by the author as follows: theologoumenon is "a theological assertion that does not directly express a matter of faith or an official teaching of the Church, and hence is in itself not normative, but that expresses in language that may prescind from factuality a notion which supports, enhances, or is related to a matter of faith" (p. 548).

Brown took note[4] of Fitzmyer's paper to point out that his basic view is being upheld by others. He disagrees with Fitzmyer, however, in the understanding of Lk's infancy narrative. Brown maintains that Luke is a witness to the belief on Mary's virginal maternity, which is called into question by Fitzmyer.

At a certain point in his booklet (footnote 9), Brown states in explicit terms that he welcomes criticism of this and other positions of his. He cautions, however, that to question a scholar's faith or his intentions is scarcely a scholarly discussion. I understand this to mean that the author accepts criticism on the forum of scholarship and scientific analysis. If this writer takes up the subject of Mary's virginity as it appears in the New Testament, it is certainly not in order to deal with the problem of Brown's personal faith. This is not a problem for me to discuss, let alone to judge or to decide. Neither is it my purpose to pass criticism on anyone.

My purpose is positive. Brown's and Fitzmyer's reflections and the problem that they think is unsolved, prompted me to read again the New Testament with their problem in my own mind, in an effort to contrast their positions, not with some texts, but with the general attitude of the New Testament in this regard. The thoughts this re-reading suggested to me are formulated in the pages that follow. In my discussion the New Testament is not regarded as a theological document but it is rather viewed from the angle of the *historical* contribution it can give to the subject under discussion. It would seem appropriate to follow a chronological order; in this case Paul

4 Brown R., 'Note. Luke's Description of the Virginal Conception', *TheolStud* 35 (1974) 360–362.

would come first. Since in the Gospels, however, though written after Paul's literature, the earliest traditions concerning Jesus Himself are preserved, they are given the first place. The infancy narratives in Mt and Lk are treated separately. A last section deals with various concepts related to the problem.

THE SILENCE OF THE NEW TESTAMENT

It is generally agreed that, except for Mt and Lk, in the entire New Testament no clear statement is found which could amount to an explicit admission of the virginal conception of Jesus. At any rate, nothing is found which could be compared with the accounts in Mt and Lk. This fact is clear and the agreement, therefore, is not surprising.

But how to read this fact? One first point is how the silence of the New Testament on this matter is to be interpreted. This silence has often been understood as ignorance, if not denial, of the belief on Jesus' virgin birth. Sometimes, however, it so happens that silence, far from being mute, is rather eloquent.

Another point is whether the New Testament is absolutely silent about the matter itself, even when it is granted that any explicit statement about such a matter is missing. It may happen that one works or writes on an assumption—never stated because it is supposed to be common knowledge—which occasionally shines through a casual word or sentence that betrays an unintentional reference to the underlying assumption. These casual references, should they exist, would be all the more valuable, precisely because they would be above any suspicion of atheological, polemic or apologetic interest and manipulation. This is why the silence of the New Testament is taken up in the first place. It may prove important and eloquent.

With many others, both Brown and Fitzmyer feel that the silence of the New Testament (except for Mt and Lk) does not boost the historicity of the virginal conception. "The NT material that rests in some way on apostolic witness . . . offers *no support* for the virginal conception" (B., p. 59). Fitzmyer's conclusion agrees: "The upshot of the investigation of the earliest Gospel is that it too has no clear affirmation of a Christian belief in the virginal conception of Jesus" (p. 558).

The argument *ex silentio* is easy to unsheath but not so easy to handle.[5] It can be conclusively used only when one can prove that a given person could not help talking or writing about that which is passed over in silence. To provide this proof is mostly virtually impossible. In the particular case of Mk it is obvious that the evangelist begins his Gospel with the ministry of John the Baptist and the Baptism of Christ, and the work ends with the Ascension of the Lord. Nothing concerning the non-public life of Christ is represented in Mk, and this also applies to the so-called infancy narratives which, in Mk and Lk, record the origins of Jesus, particularly, for our purpose, his virginal conception. The scope within which Mk had decided to contain his narrative is the *public* ministry of Christ, "from the baptism of John to the day he (Christ) was taken up from us" (Acts 1, 22), which is in perfect agreement with the area that the earliest Christian Church had normatively decided to cover in her missionary preaching (Acts 1, 12f; 10, 37ff; 13, 23ff; etc.)—which is also the scope of the other three Gospels, in spite of their additions at the beginning. The goal the evangelist had set for

---

[5] Interesting and instructive reflections on the theological value of the alleged silence in some writings of the NT concerning our problem, can be seen in Rahner Karl, 'Dogmatische Bemerkunken zur Jungfrauengeburt', in *Zum Thema Jungfrauengeburt* (Stuttgart, 1970) 212ff.

himself could explain abundantly why other information beyond these bounds could or should be omitted. It is all the more so if this other information was not considered essential to, or integral part of, the "gospel of Jesus Christ" (Mk 1, 1), as it is the view of many scholars.[6] Brown agrees.[7] One cannot use the silence of Mk to conclude that he was ignorant of the virginal conception of Jesus and other related stories.

Silence About Any Human Father

But beyond that, one can raise the question as to whether the silence of Mark on this matter is so absolute that it offers 'no support' for the virginal conception. Some elements seem to tilt the balance in the other direction.

It is worth noticing that Joseph, Mary's husband, is completely ignored by Mk; he does not even mention the name. One of the implications is that Mary is not related to any husband—and still she is "the mother" of Jesus in Mk (3, 31), and Jesus is "the son of Mary" (6, 3) and of Mary alone. Another implication, which is more relevant for us at this moment, is that Joseph does not appear as Jesus' father. What is more, the evangelist does not know of any human father of Jesus; he *never* mentions the notion "father" or "son" to link Jesus to some human father; he *never* suggests or hints that any man is father of Jesus; there are indicative elements in Mk (see below) to maintain that the evangelist carefully and deliberately shuns relating Jesus to any human paternity. Though Jesus is "the son of Mary," he appears to be the son of no man, of no immediate father. He may be "son of David" (Mk 10, 48f; cfr 12, 35, 37; 11, 10), but he is not a "ben-Joseph" for Mk. Except for Mk 6, 3, in this Gospel Jesus is usually identified, not by any family name like ben-Joseph, but by his home-town: he is

[6] Cfr Béda Rigaux, 'Sense et portée de Mc 3, 31–35 dans la Mariologie neotestamentaire', in *Maria in Sacra Scriptura* (Acta congressus Mariologici-Mariani in Republica Dominicana . . ., IV), (Rome, 1967) 531.

[7] Brown R., 'The Virginal Conception,' 58.

Jesus the Nazarene (1, 24; 10, 47; 14, 67; 16, 6; cfr 1, 9; 6, 1).

It is against the missing human fatherhood of Jesus that another detail in this Gospel is striking. In a passage difficult for other reasons, Mk puts on the lips of Jesus himself the following statement: about that day no one knows, neither the angels "nor the Son—except the Father" (Mk 13, 32). Besides the fact that the Son appears as superior to the angels (notice the gradation), the absolute expressions "the Son, the Father" are highly significant. Such a phrasing has a Johannine ring to it, and links the Markan expressions—which remain unique in Mk—to the likewise unique passage in Mt 11, 27 and parallel Lk 10, 22 (the "Johannine *logion*") the original authenticity of which was strenuously defended by Jeremias.[8] For Mk Christ is simply "the" Son as over against "the" Father. In other words, the father of Christ (the Son) is the Father, i.e. God.[9] Again, in Mk 8, 38 the evangelist has Christ Himself say that the Son of Man will come in the glory of "his" Father, accompanied by the holy angels—where the serving role of angels is to be noticed. In the parable of the perfidious vinedressers it is again Christ Himself who says that, after many "servants" the Owner of the vineyard still had one left, "a beloved son"; he thought that they would respect "my son," who was "the" heir (12, 6f). It is in Mk (12, 35ff) also that we see Christ applying to Himself the oracle of the Old Testament:[10] "Yahweh said to my Lord: sit

[8] Jeremias Joachim, *The Prayers of Jesus* (Studies in Biblical Theology. Second Series 6), (Naperville, 1967) 45ff.

[9] Cfr Jeremias J., *The Prayers*, 36f: Son, Father, "both used absolutely, stand side by side, *ho hyiós* used in this way is a christological title which became established rather late in the history of the early church . . . Only in the Johannine literature does it come to the fore. As *ho hyiós* used absolutely in this way as a title is not a designation for the Messiah in Palestinian linguistic usage, Mark 13, 32 can have reached its present form only in the context of the Hellenistic community."

[10] Interpreted as messianic already in Judaism before Christ: cfr Strack H.-Billerbeck P., *Kommentar zum Neuen Testament*, IV/1 (München, 1928) 452, 458f. Cfr recently Neugebauer Fritz, 'Die Davidssohnfrage (Mark

at my right hand" (Ps 110, 1; cfr Mk 14, 62). On the basis of
this text Christ challenges the Jewish exegesis of it: "David
himself calls him (the Messiah) *lord;* how, therefore, can
he be *his* son?" The suggestion is obvious: Christ is "son" of
somebody else, superior to David, i.e. son of Yahweh.[11] In the
transfiguration narrative (Mk 9, 7) the "voice from the clouds"
declares that "this is my Son, the beloved one." Again "the
voice from heaven" addressing Jesus at His baptism states that
"you are my son, the beloved one, in you I am well pleased"
(Mk 1, 11); later on, when Jesus was tempted, He was "served"
(cfr Mk 1, 10, 43–45) by the angels (see a similar contrast in
Hebr. 1, 5, 6–9). In His prayer in Gethsemane Jesus addresses
God as *"Abba, Father."*[12] Significantly enough, all these passages where Jesus appears as the son of some father report words
of Christ or of God, the implication being that the evangelist
certainly accepts and adopts the view of the texts. Besides the
foregoing passages, the evil spirits also acknowledge Christ as
'the son of God' or as "the son of God the most high" in Mk 3,

XII, 35–7 parr.) und der Menschensohn,' *NTS* 21 (1974) 88, who maintains that 'the suggestion of Jesus doubtlessly takes for granted that his
opponents also explain the passage messianically.' The Jewish silence about
the messianic meaning of Ps 110 between 100 and 250 A.D. (when it is
referred to Abraham of Ezekiah) is, he understands, an antichristian reaction.
'The fact that this reasoning (on Ps 110) is profusedly interspersed in the
New Testament and the Jewish silence until 100 speak a clear language'
(fnt 8). The author understands that, according to Mt and Mk, in an
exstatic vision ('in Spirit') David saw in heaven and heard 'what God, the
Lord, says to his Lord, and, therefore, this Lord is a Lord who is in immediate nearness to God, who is seated at God's right hand' (89); which is a
reference to 'the dignity of him of whom David spoke and whom Jesus
meant'—even though the author points to the figure of the Son of Man 'who
shares God's power and dignity' (107). This kind of dialectic process is
traced back to John the Baptist (101–106).

[11] Cf *Barn.* 12 11: 'See how David calls him Lord and does not call him
son.' Cannot a similar suggestion be detected in Mk 10:18 (only one is
good)?

[12] Cfr Jeremias J., *The Prayers,* 62: ". . . Jesus never allies himself with
his disciples in saying 'Our Father' when he prays, and distinguishes between
'my Father' and 'your Father' in what he says. This consistent distinction
shows that what we established in the case of the saying is also true of the
prayers of Jesus: Jesus' use of *abba* expresses a special relationship with
God."

11; 5, 7 (cfr 1, 24). Even the Roman soldier concludes that "this man was son of God" (15, 39).

It is against this background that the particular problem in Mk 1, 1 should be evaluated. The Gospel of Mk opens with this title or statement of purpose: "Beginning of the gospel of Jesus Christ, *Son of God.*" There is some textual uncertainty concerning the words 'Son of God,' because they are omitted in some witnesses of the textual tradition. But an objective and dispassionate evaluation of the external evidence would certainly decide in favor of the words in question. A glance at the critical apparatus will show that the support for the words (in some form) outweighs the support of their omission, both in quantity and in quality. As for the internal evidence, the above mentioned texts are clear evidence that Mk certainly shared the view expressed by the reading "Son of God" and that he very often discloses this view throughout the Gospel with almost the same words.[13] There is little doubt that the reading should be maintained. Modern translations, in fact, keep the reading.[14] The implication is that right at the beginning of his Gospel Mark points out that Jesus Christ is "Son of God." This is how he introduces Jesus to his readers; such is His identity: this man is "son of God," not "son of Joseph" or of any other man. This certainly agrees with and is linked to the fact that Mark, throughout his Gospel, fails to introduce Christ as the son of Joseph—though he can occasionally be presented as "the son of Mary" and Mary can be said to be "his mother."

It is certainly striking that Mk *never* relates Jesus to any human father—even more, he is careful to prevent such an understanding,—whereas he shows an obvious insistence on the definition of Christ as son of God. One wonders whether this

---

[13] Schweizer Eduard, *Das Evangelium nach Markus,* (Das NT Deutsch 1), (Göttingen, 1967) 15, favors the view that the reading is a later addition, "in agreement, however, with Mark's general language."

[14] *The New American Bible; The New English Bible. The Jerusalem Bible* (both in French and English) keeps the words in the text, but cautions: "omit 'the Son of God.' "

can be explained by sheer chance, if chance has ever been the explanation of anything at all. The absolute ignorance of Mark about Joseph as well as the ignorance about any human father of Jesus (even in 6, 3) as over against the insistence on God as father of Jesus (and of Jesus as son of God) seem to be a clear indication that a set design of the evangelist is at work here, and that he is perfectly aware of what he writes and of what he fails to write. According to this design in Mk, Jesus remains the son of Mary and the son of God *exclusively*. This is the fact. If the evangelist's awareness of this fact is rejected, some other convincing explanation of the fact has to be provided—which does not seem to be an easy task.

It can be argued that the title "son of God" which Christ is given in Mk is just a messianic title, without any implications concerning Jesus' origins and personality. Such a view, however, does not explain the general perspective of Mk.[15] It does not explain, in the first place, his total ignorance of Joseph or of any human paternity for Christ (as over against God's paternity), whereas a human maternity is clearly admitted—and this fact certainly calls for some explanation other than chance. It does not explain, in the second place, the *absolute* use of "the Son" (not "son of God") over against the absolute "the Father" (Mk 13, 32) with its Johannine flavor.[16] This passage is evidence of a deep Christological insight concerning the very per-

---

[15] That the Son does not know about 'that day' is no objection against this understanding. Even in the highly-developed Christology of John, the Father is 'greater' than the Son (Jn 14, 28); the Son 'cannot' do anything of His own (5:19, 30); He does not do anything of His own but according to what the Father 'teaches' Him (8:28); the Father 'commands' Him what to say, the Son does not speak of His own (12:49f); Jesus is not the source of His own doctrine but "my doctrine is not mine but of him who sent me" (7:16). These expressions indicate some sort of restriction.

[16] Schweizer E., *Das Evangelium nach Markus*, 162: Whereas (the title) Son of God, in contraposition to son of a human father, is an expression of Highness, the absolute expression 'the Son' always leads one to think of the opposite 'the Father'; it describes *a priori*, therefore, a subordinate position in reference to the Father . . . he (the Son) is not a second God, but he in whom the one God turns his face to the world."

son of Christ; it goes far beyond any messianic title, which, incidentally, is nowhere attested in this absolute form.[17] This deep insight is clearly suggested when Mk (12, 36f) has Christ maintain that the merely Davidic sonship of the Messiah does not explain the terms of the oracle "Yahweh said to my Lord" (Ps 110, 1)—another passage of Mk which is not explained by the assumption of just a messianic title, since the very purpose of the passage is a higher form of "sonship" of the Messiah.[18] After all, Mk's Gospel was composed long after Paul had written that, before His *kenosis,* Christ had enjoyed a pre-existence in which He was "rich" and lived in "the form of God, being equal to God" (2 Cor 8, 9; Phil 2, 6). The presence of Paulinisms in Mk (v. gr. Mk, 10, 45) has been established long ago.[19]

On the other hand, modern biblical scholarship has acquainted us with several "Sitze" of the Gospel material. Whatever the meaning of the voice from heaven (1, 11; 9, 7) or of the evil spirits (3, 11; 5, 7; cfr 1, 24 with Jn 6, 69) within the context of Jesus' lifetime, the meaning of the same expressions within the context of the faith of the Church of the evangelist at the

[17] Cfr footnote 9.

[18] Schweizer E., *Das Evangelium nach Mk,* 147: "Step by step the community recognizes Jesus' mystery. Where or when was this or that stated is not decisive, but this: whether or not what is said adequately describes the reality of Jesus. Hence this is to be said: that, in fact, Mk 12: 36f sees what is decisive, and that the formulation reaches its last sharpness and power in Paul (Rom 1:3; Gal 4, 4f; cfr 3: 3), where these two ideas are held fast: that God from all eternity and for all eternity is God for us in the 'Son,' and still this his being-for-us lives in the man Jesus within history. Mark felt, quite rightly, that it is here that the boundary between scribes and Jesus' community is reached."

[19] The view of this writer is not that Mk was directly influenced by Paul's theology, nor is it that Paul is the discover of all so-called Paulinisms. The contention is rather that even Paul is indebted to the common Christian faith which developed and grew both before and side by side with Paul's theology. Concerning v. gr. Christ's pre-existence cfr Schweizer E., 'Zur Herkunft der Präexistenzvorstellung bei Paulus,' *Neotestamentica* (Zürich/Stuttgart, 1963) 109: some pre- and post-Pauline passages in the NT "show that the concept (of pre-existence) also exists in the community both before and side by side with Paul."

time the Gospel was written is certainly different, i.e. richer and deeper. In fact, it is in the light of the foregoing passages (13, 32; 12, 36f) that these other texts just mentioned should be read: they represent the faith of Mk's community and of Mark himself, rather than that of the evil spirits, etc. This is particularly true of the introductory statement in Mk 1, 1, where the evangelist expresses his own view.

Some other details support this understanding. The "son of God" to whom Mk refers is the Christ who was "raised" from the dead and "is not here" any longer (16, 6); he is the son of God who will come "in the glory of *his Father*" (8, 38), with power and much glory (13, 26), and will be seated "at the right hand of the Power" (14, 62); He is superior to the angels who are His courtiers (8, 38), His envoys (13, 27), and "serve" Him (1, 13; cfr 13, 32); He appears as supreme lord of nature whose presence causes "a great fear" (4, 41), which obviously is a theophanic fear (cfr 9, 6); He has absolute power over evil spirits and can give this power to others (3, 24ff.15; 6, 7.12); He can forgive sins, and "who can forgive sins except God alone?" (2, 10.7); He is "the heir" of the vineyard, the "beloved son" of the Owner and far superior to all "servants" (12, 3ff); He is a "son of God" who, in prayer, addresses God as "Abba, Father" (14, 36)—the only instance in Mk where any one addresses God as Father and where the original Abba is preserved.

When all these details *taken together* are viewed in the light of the "the Son" who relates to "the Father" in absolute terms (13, 22) and of the Messiah who can hardly be "son" of David on account of His relationship to Yahweh (12, 36f), there can be little doubt that Mk's understanding of expressions like "the son of God," "my son" or "his Father" goes far beyond the meaning of a merely messianic title;[20] particularly so when one realizes that most of the time such statements are placed precisely on God's or on Christ's lips. The Christ of the Christian

20 Cfr Schweizer E., *Das Evangelium nach Mk,* 207.

community—of Mk's community—is far more than the Jewish Messiah. And it is against the background of this belief that for Mk Christ is "the son of Mary" and "the son of God"—whereas no mention is made of any human paternity of Jesus.

Jesus, "The Son of Mary"

Let us come closer to our subject now. It is well known that in the episode of Jesus' appearance in the synagogue of His home-town, Nazareth, His countrymen are surprised by His performance: "Is not this the carpenter, *the son of Mary* and brother of James, of Joseph, of Judas and of Simon? Are not his sisters here among us?"[21] Obviously, this is an important statement in our discussion.

The textual evidence presents two other alternative readings for "the carpenter, the son of Mary": a) the son of the carpenter (from Mt 13, 35); b) the son of the carpenter and of Mary (Mt and Mk combined). There is no need to waste any time on this, since the evidence in favor of either alternative reading is negligible when compared with the overwhelming textual support for the reading offered in the first place. There is almost unanimous agreement on this both among the critical editors of the New Testament and in commentaries, for reasons both external and internal.[22] Taylor maintains the reading 'the son of the carpenter' because—he reasons—the overwhelmingly attested reading "implies a knowledge of the Virgin Birth tradition."[23] Obviously this is no scholarly reason to support such a reading—nor is it an honest reason.

[21] As for the question about Jesus' brothers and sisters it does not pose any real problem in the subject under discussion. Cfr recently Blinzler Josef, *Die Brüder und Schwestern Jesu* (Stuttgarter Bibelstudien 21), (Stuttgart 2d, ed., 1967).

[22] Cfr Rigaux Béda, 'Sense et portée,' 532f; Segbroeck Frans van, 'Jésus rejeté par sa patrie (Mt 13, 54–58),' *Bib* 49 (1968) 181f.

[23] Taylor Vincent, *The Text of the New Testament. A Short Introduction* (London 2d. ed., 1963); *id., The Gospel according to St. Mark* (London, 1957) 299f. McArthur Harvey K., 'Son of Mary,' *NovTest* 15 (1973) 47ff, would incline to accept this reading but he admits this is his "own suspicion" (52).

Interestingly enough, however, in Taylor's view the well-attested reading implies Mary's virginity—which is not necessarily so when the text is looked at superficially. In fact, when, against the Jewish custom, someone is identified not by his father but by his mother, the implication could be an irregular paternity;[24] and the expression on the lips of the Nazareth crowds could signify an insult against Jesus (cfr Jn 8, 18.41; 9, 29). Or, again, the identification "the son of Mary" could suggest that Joseph was dead; the example in Lk 7, 12 is illustrative.[25]

Still, the text of Mk "this is the carpenter, the son of Mary" has to be read against a broader background and on a broader basis. The phrase is placed on the lips of the crowds even in Mk, so that the view expressed by it does not necessarily represent the view of the evangelist. At any rate, the context does not provide any clues for an insulting intention: the purpose of vv. 2 and 3 is to stress that Jesus was just like everybody else in town, with nothing extraordinary or outstanding about Him. Mk introduces the girl of 7, 25 as the daughter of her mother only; in Mk 15, 40.47; 16, 1 some people are related only to their mother. There is no reason to assume an irregular paternity, and certainly not an insulting intention in the evangelist. It is to be pointed out, however, that if, in fact, the expression of the crowds were to be understood as an insult, this would be highly telling in regard to our discussion—and the perspec-

[24] Not necessarily though: cfr Blinzler J., *Brüder*, 71f. This is, however, what seems to be implied by Stauffer Ethelbert, 'Jeschu Ben Mirjam. Kontroversgeschichtliche Anmerkungen zu Mk 6: 3,' *Neotestamentica et Semitica*, (Festschrift for Matthew Black), ed. Ellis E.-Willcox M. (Edinburgh, 1969) 119–128: "Only Mark had the courage to repeat" the insulting name Jesus, son of Mary (122). Still McArthur H., 'Son of Mary,' 45, contends "that in the case of the Old Testament and Rabbinic literature it is difficult to demonstrate that this practice was followed," and that such an explanation for Mk 6: 13 raises many questions (p. 52c). His own view, however, that Mk 6: 3 'may' be explained on the assumption of an 'informal description' faces the textual problem of Mt, Lk and Jn agreeing against Mk.

[25] Other examples in Blinzler J., *Brüder*, 72. Cfr Schweizer E. *ThWNT* VIII 364: "Offenbar ist Joseph früh verstorben," with others mentioned in the footnote.

tive of a virginal conception should be left wide open. The assumption, on the other hand, that Joseph was dead at the time would render somewhat more acceptable Jesus' identity as "the son of Mary"; but, as rightly pointed out by Rigaux,[26] it is an "unverifiable conjecture. . . ." Here as in the rest of the Gospel Mark just ignores Joseph.

But is it true that concerning this expression "the son of Mary" Mk is a detached reporter handing down the crowds' *ipsissima verba?* The problem is one of literary analysis. The Markan text under consideration is one belonging to the general synoptic tradition, and, as such, it is paralleled by both Mt and Lk. The phrasing of Mt 13, 55 is this: "Isn't this the carpenter's son? Isn't his mother called Mary and his brothers James, Joseph, Simon and Judas? And are not all his sisters among us?" Lk's text (4, 22) is much shorter: "Is not this Joseph's son?"

It is obvious that in the narrative of apparently the same episode of the synagogue, from a literary point of view Lk (4, 16–30) has almost nothing in common with Mk. His is a clearly independent narrative. Still, it contains the above mentioned expression which is parallel to Mk (though the meaning is different: admiration, praise). The odds are that such a phrase came to Lk through some channels other than Mk. In the first place, no reasonable explanation can be offered as to the question why did Luke change the Markan text, "*the* son of Mary," into "son of Joseph." After his infancy narratives where Lk insists on Mary's virginal conception through the Spirit, this evangelist had every reason to preserve the Markan text. Notice that in 3, 23 he takes care to point out in one of his own remarks, that Jesus "was, *as was supposed*, son of Joseph." The contention that Lk changed Mk's phrasing in order to substantiate the "supposition" in 3, 23, can be twisted, in the sense that such a remark in

---

[26] 'Sense et portée,' 544. Furthermore, McArthur H., 'Son of Mary,' 44, in regard to the view that the son of a widow was identified by his mother's name, notes that "This is an understandable piece of speculative logic. Unfortunately the evidence in support of it is less than substantial," both in the OT and in rabbinic literature.

3, 23 was written in view of, and in preparation for, the popular opinion expressed in 4, 22. On the other hand, if Lk's source offered a text like that in Mt, it is difficult to explain why he should omit that Jesus was son of Mary.

Furthermore, the fact that in Lk 4, 22 Christ is regarded as Joseph's son shows that the failure of this evangelist to mention the brothers and sisters of Jesus is not due to any concern to dispel any suspicion or doubt about Mary's virginity. Additional proof for this is that in 8, 19–21 (and Acts 1, 14) Lk does mention Jesus' "brothers" who accompany "his mother." No easy explanation, moreover, can be given why Lk should pass over in silence that Jesus was a carpenter (alternatively, son of the carpenter, Mt), if this were to be taken to mean a lack of a respectable status, after the same evangelist had written that the best Jesus could be offered for a cradle was a manger (2, 7)— which becomes a "sign" (2, 12.16)—and, that Joseph's and Mary's offering in the temple was that of the poor (2, 25; Lev 12, 8). On the other hand, the Lukan text that Jesus is "son of Joseph" (ben-Joseph) is in perfect agreement with the Jewish identification practice; it is a more acceptable text from a historical viewpoint.[27]

These reasons indicate that this text of Lk can be convincingly accounted for only on the assumption that Lk in this narrative does not depend on Mk[28] but follows some other source, prob-

---

[27] McArthur H., 'Son of Mary,' 38, quotes b. Yebamoth 54b: " . . . and only a father's family may be called the proper family." Additional references are: b. Baba Bathra 109b, 110a, b. Kiddushim 69a. Sifre Num 114.

[28] Anderson Hugh, 'Broadening Horizons. The Rejection at Nazareth Pericope in Luke 4, 16–30 in light of Recent Critical trends,' *Interpretation* 18 (1964) 275, notes that the history of interpretation of this passage in Lk does show that it is difficult both theologically and literarily—particularly so literarily, if it is considered as an elaboration of Mk 6, 1ff. Dodd C. H., *Historical Tradition in the Fourth Gospel* (Cambridge, 1965) 240, fnt 1: ". . . it appears that the Lukan account of the incident in the synagogue at Nazareth . . . is entirely independent of Mark." Finkel Asher, 'Jesus' Sermon at Nazareth, Luc 4, 16–30,' *Abraham Unser Vater* (Festschr. for O. Michel), (Leiden/Köln, 1963) 115: "Thus, we may conclude that Luke (and John 4, 44) represents the earlier narrative of rejection and astonishment at Jesus' home-town at the beginning of his ministry. Whereas Mark and

ably the Q source which is common to Mt also. This source, therefore, reported that the "people" in Nazareth, following their customary usage, identified Jesus as "son of Joseph," not as "the son of Mary." The Q source is held to be considerably older than Mk.

The narrative of the synagogue episode in Mt 13, 53–58 is manifestly based on the narrative of Mk 6, 1–6.[29] But it is obvious that in v. 55 Mt adds another source to Mk and combines both to build his own text. In fact, Mt also had every reason to preserve the Markan text ('the son of Mary') after he had insisted on Mary's virginal conception (1, 18–25) and that is why no compelling reason could drive him to change or correct the Markan text. And yet, while preserving the general

---

Matthew record a narrative of rejection on a later date." John Dominic, 'Mark and the Relatives of Jesus,' *NovTest* 15 (1973) 101, points out that "only Joseph is mentioned so that Lk IV 22 can hardly be derived from Mk VI 3. In the case of Jn VI 42 . . . both parents are mentioned. Whatever relationship might exist between Lk IV 22 and Jn VI 42 it is obvious that there are traces of some contrast between genealogy and genius in the tradition outside of Mark. It is to be assumed from this that Mark found VI 2b–3 in his received tradition."—Bajard J., 'La structure de la péricope de Nazareth en Lc. IV, 16–30,' *EphTheolLov* 45 (1969) 165–171, argues convincingly for the literary unity of the entire passage: "If Luke has used sources, the seams are at any rate hardly visible" (171)—against Bultmann Rudolf K., *The History of the Synoptic Tradition* (English trans. by Marsh John), (Oxford, 1968) 31f. But it is Schürmann H., 'Zur Traditionsgeschichte der Nazareth-Perikope Lk 4, 16–30,' *Mélanges Bibliques en hommage au R. P. Béda Rigaux* (Gembloux, 1970) 186–205, who devoted a thorough analysis to this discussion to conclude that "Luke had found a variation of the Nazareth pericope which also came to Mk . . . the basic part of that pre-Lukan pericope (behind Lk 4: 16, 22, 23b, 24 . . .) in not a few places preserved a form older than Mk 6, 1–6 . . . Matthew also read the narrative attested by Lk 4, 14f. 16–30 in the same sequence, and indeed—as Luke—in the *Redequelle*," i.e. the Q source (which he shows in pps. 200–204). In p. 195 the author maintains "that the original part of the pericope —which can be seen behind Lk vv. 16.22.23–24 (28ff)—cannot be understood as a redaction of Mk by Lk; Luke has already received the expanded pericope from a non-Markan *Vorlage*." That v. 22, in particular, is not a creation by Lk is shown in p. 196.

29 Though mentioning different opinions, Segbroeck Frans van, 'Jésus' rejeté,' 168, informs us that "contemporary exegetes in general decide in favor of Mt's dependence from Mk"; in spite of the fact that Vaganay maintains Mt's independence (*ibid.*, 182). "Mt's dependence from Mk is beyond question" (p. 197).

character of Mk's text, he inserts a detail into it in which Mt
agrees with Lk, namely, that Jesus is "the" son of Joseph, though
Joseph is presented as a "carpenter"[30]—a term taken from Mk,
where it applies to Jesus. Mt was prompted to do so in order
to preserve another element of the Gospel tradition found in
the Q source. Then, from Mk he keeps the mention of Mary—
no longer in the form "the son of Mary" but in the form "his
mother is called Mary." The text of Mt is by no means original
as its dependence on Mk is only too obvious. But it is still
relevant because his text is witness to another source where, in
the same episode, Christ appeared as the son of Joseph; it is
the source that Luke follows. This is one of the cases in which
Mt and Lk agree against Mk. But there is more. The fourth
Gospel expresses the popular amazement in these terms: "Is
not this (man) Jesus the son of Joseph (i.e. 'Jesus ben-Joseph')
whose father and mother we know?"[31] (cfr Jn 1, 45 also). This
view is expressed in a "synagogue," that of Capharnaum (6, 59).
The other themes of the synagogue episode in the synoptics are
preserved by John also, but they are scattered throughout his
Gospel (4, 44; 7, 15). To Jesus' brothers reference is made in
Jn 2, 12; 7, 2.5. The fourth Gospel represents a tradition
independent from the synoptics, which on this point of Jesus'
identity agrees with Lk and Mt while disagreeing with Mk. The
implication is that the Johannine tradition goes back to an early
stage to reach, beyond Mk, the same strand of tradition which
is behind Lk and Mt. The agreement of Lk, Mt and Jn is a
formidable coalition that not even Mk can stand.

The conclusion is that the earlier and, therefore, more original
evangelic tradition concerning the synagogue episode under
analysis identified Jesus as son of Joseph, as a "ben-Joseph,"

---

[30] The name "Joseph," however, appears in respectable early translations
such as the Syriac Sinaitic, Syriac Curetonian and the "Itala."

[31] Notice that 'and mother' is missing in such outstanding witnesses as
the Sinaiticus in its original hand, the Freerianus, the Old Syriac version
(both the Sinaitic and the Curetonian), an important manuscript (Veronen-
sis) of the Itala and some others.

which is the most obvious and historically reliable identification also.[32] It is this realization that explains the coalition of both the synoptic tradition as represented by Mt and Lk as well as the Johannine tradition, against Mk.

The implication is simple but significant. It is Mk who intervenes in the traditional material.[33] It is he who "changes" the traditional identification of Jesus from "son of Joseph" into "the son of Mary." What is more, on the evidence of Lk 4, 22, who omits any mention of Mary or of the "mother," and of Jn 6, 42, who mentions the "mother" but not her name, one may say that it was Mk who introduced the name of Mary and of her motherly relationship to Jesus into the synagogue episode.

On the other hand, while Mk intervenes in some "traditional" material,[34] he does not invent the episode. Evidence for this is: that the episode itself with its main themes is found in the independent narrative of Lk 4, 16–30; the parallel episode in Jn 6, 42, which also takes place in a "synagogue" where Jesus was

---

[32] And even the possibility of an Aramaism has been mentioned: cfr Schürman H., 'Zur Traditionsgeschichte' 197 and fnt 3. At any rate, "Luke did not read the *son of Joseph* in Mk," the author maintains.

[33] Segbroeck F., 'Jésus rejeté,' 195f: in Mk 6: 1–6 "several indications of this evangelist's redactional activity are perceived. At the same time, however, many an indication of his dependence from his source is found . . . we do not think that Mk's dependence from an earlier tradition is in any way doubtful." Crossan J. D., 'Mark,' 102, who does not consider our topic in any way, very recently from his analysis comes to the result that "it must be concluded that Mark is positively uninterested in the father of Jesus while being quite interested in his mother, brothers and sisters. It is this phenomenon which suggests a solution to the problem of Mk VI 3 in relation to Mt XIII 55. The argument is that: 1) the questioning reaction . . . of the home-town in the basic tradition noted Jesus' profession, Jesus' father and mother by name, and Jesus' brothers and sisters; 2) *the name of Joseph as the most normal and important way of denoting human origins, was retained in the abbreviated tradition behind Lk IV 22 and Jn VI 42;* 3) *it was deliberately erased by Mark himself as part of the positive uninterest just noted;* 4) Mt XIII 35 in following Mark does not accept this strange genealogical note and so changes Jesus' profession into an indication of paternity which makes the minimal change necessary in his source—but still does not name the father; 5) *Mark's redactional change in VI 2b–3 was the removal of Jesus' named father from the text"* (italics mine throughout).

[34] Which, according to Crossan J. D., 'Mark,' 99–105, was restricted to vv. 2b–4a, but it is a "traditional datum" all the same.

'teaching' (v. 59; cfr Mk 6, 2) which represent the main elements put together by Mk in his narrative, plus Jn 2, 12; 7, 2.5 which mention Jesus' brothers; some linguistic details in the text of Mk such as the following: the interrogative formulation of the sentence, just as in Lk and Jn; the clause *ouch houtos estin . . . ho hyios* which is found in practically the same form in the *independent* traditions of Lk and Jn also; the peculiar name *Ioses* in Mk (6, 3; 15, 40.17)—changed into *Ioseph* by Mt,—when the same evangelist also knows the usual name Ioseph (15, 43.45).[35]

As a result, Mk does not appear as a detached reporter. He changes the traditional material, and this change no doubt represents his own thought, a definite intention of this evangelist. Obviously, this change could not be meant as an insult. The assumption that he changed the text because Joseph was already dead is no explanation at all when we realize that not only Lk but also Jn keep the name of Joseph—and not that of Mary— long after Mk was written.

The only reason one can think of why Mk departed from the older and otherwise uniform phrasing of the tradition, and why he makes a deliberate effort to eliminate any mention of Joseph at this point, is the same reason which impelled him not to mention Joseph in his entire Gospel, to exclude any human paternity of Jesus, to omit that Mary had any husband—and to insist on the fact that Jesus is "son of God." In other words, the reason of his change is his conviction that Jesus is "son of Mary" and "son of God" *exclusively*.[36]

---

[35] Cfr *id., ibid.*, 108.

[36] Schürmann H., 'Zur Traditionsgeschichte,' 197, maintains that "the completely unusual identification of Jesus after his mother in Mk 6, 3, can be in reference to the faith of the community in the virgin birth; at any rate, it cannot be regarded as more original than the formulation in Lk 4, 22." Bultmann R., *Die Geschichte der synoptischen Tradition,* (Göttingen, 6th edition, 1964) 16, 'Ergänzungsheft' 9, notes the knowledge "that she (Mary) was venerated as the Mother of the Lord" can be behind the formulation of Mk 6: 3 (in the better attested reading).

A Mother, But No Father

This conviction of the evangelist is further evidenced by some other detail in his Gospel. It is the passage Mk 3, 31–35, where, in reference to Jesus, the evangelist reports that 'his mother and his brothers' came to Him, and Christ states that "any one who does the will of God, this is my brother and sister and mother." We meet here a preliminary textual problem. In v. 32 to Jesus' mother and brothers the evangelist also adds "your sisters." Notice that three times, in vv. 31.33.34, the evangelist mentions "your mother and your brothers" only. Except for the conclusion in v. 35 (see below), the addition "and your sisters" is found in v. 32 only. Now, this addition in v. 32 has a weak support in the textual transmission, whereas the omission of "and your sisters" is overwhelmingly backed by the textual evidence—to the point that the modern critical edition by Kurt Alland and others takes this reading out of the text. Luke (8; 20, a parallel passage) also fails to mention the sisters, and his failure cannot be explained by dogmatic qualms (Mary's virginity) since he mentions the brothers. In the parallel passage of Mt 12, 47 the entire verse is in a very bad form, from a text-criticism viewpoint; but, how it may help, it also omits the mention of sisters. On the other hand, the addition in Mk 3, 32 can be explained by the presence of "sister" in v. 35, where it is authentic. The conclusion is that the mention of sisters in v. 32 has to be discarded, in agreement with the entire section, both before and after v. 32, until the conclusion in v. 35.[37]

This passage presents a literary problem also. Whereas the parallel text in Mt 12, 46–50 reproduces almost literally (except, perhaps, for v. 47) the text of Mk, the text in Lk is considerably shorter. But, more to the point, Luke never mentions

---

[37] Cfr Blinzler J., *Brüder*, 21: in v. 32 " 'his sisters' is an obvious interpolation on the basis of 3, 35 and 6, 3."

the "sisters," not even in v. 21. This v. 21 represents the conclusion of Lk's narrative, but it is not a transcript of the present conclusion in the Markan text (v. 35). It is interesting for our purpose to notice that even in this conclusion Lk (unlike Mk) does not introduce the concept of "sisters"—thereby remaining within the terms of the entire passage, i.e. "mother and brothers."[38] On this score the Lukan conclusion does not correspond to that in Mk v. 35, but rather to the v. 34 in Mk.

In the name of modern biblical criticism I can say that the conclusion of Mk in v. 35 did not belong in this context originally. The story ended with v. 34 in Mk. It was Dibelius[39] who saw that v. 35 has been placed where it is today in order to round out the story, but it is a detached *logion* of the Lord. Rigaux[40] notes that there are good indications to support this view: the connections of the reflection about "doing God's will" in v. 35 with the foregoing story are very loose; it was the words "mother and brother" that suggested the association of v. 35 to this narrative; the asyndeton in v. 35 shows that this verse is just an accretion to the main narrative—the textual transmission betrays the grammatical uneasiness and the attempts to iron it out.[41] Crossan [42] goes as far as to hold that this v. 35 was "created" by Mk.

Recently, in a lengthy and thorough study Lambrecht, followed by Crossan,[43] contends[44] convincingly that in the entire passage Mk 3, 20–35 this evangelist is not original but follows a written source, the Q source, which is also used in Lk 11, 14–

[38] Cfr Crossan J. D., 'Mark,' 97.
[39] Dibelius Martin, *Die Formgeschichte des Evangeliums*, 5th ed. by Borkamm Günther, (Tübingen, 1966) 42f.
[40] 'Sense et Portée,' 543.
[41] Lambrecht Jan, 'Ware Verwantschap en eeuwige Zonde. Ontstaan en Structuur van Mc. 3, 20–35,' *Bijdragen* 29 (1968) 248, however, notes that asyndeton is a stylistic feature of Mk, and refers to Taylor V., *Mark,* 49f, 58, 247.
[42] Crossan J. D., 'Mark,' 97f.
[43] *Id., ibid.,* 82–98.
[44] Lambrecht J., 'Ware Verwantschap,' 114–150; 234–258; 268–393.

24 The Virgin Birth

28 independently of Mk.[45] He maintains, however, that Mk has
adjusted this source—and he has done so particularly in our
section (vv. 31–55) where Mk transforms his source very deeply
in view of Mk 6, 1–6.[46] In Lambrecht's view "the concluding
logion of Q 28 (= Lk 11, 28) and that of Mk 3, 35 must have
been one and the same logion originally" (p. 248).

Whatever the explanation, it seems that there is widespread
agreement that v. 35 represents a deliberate addition to the
foregoing story or a deliberate expansion of the saying in Lk
11, 28, which Mk found in the Q source, or a creation of the
evangelist. Lambrecht's explanation does not contradict Dibelius', but specifies it. At any rate, deliberate addition, or deliberate expansion (or both together), or creation—they certainly
indicate the thought and the views of the evangelist himself;
which remains true regardless of the soundness of literary-
critical conclusions, but the literary analysis brings the intentions of the evangelist into sharper relief.

Interestingly enough, several literary critics, not concerned
with our present discussion, point out that v. 35 in Mk was
written with Mk 6, 3 in mind.[47] This observation seems to be
irrefutable. In fact, both the parallel passage of Lk (8, 19–21),

[45] "Een direct literair kontakt tussen Mc. 3, 20–35 en Lc. 11, 14–28 bestaat
er blijkbaar niet" (237).
[46] Id., ibid.: "Enkele gegevens echter suggereren dat het aandeel van
Marcus groter is dan louter herschrijving en bewerking van een bron"
(248). "Het is inderdaad mogelijk dat het optreden der verwanten niet
teruggaat op een traditioneel gegeven, of althans niet op een geschreven bron.
Het zou ons niet verbazen dat Marcus vanuit zijn bron (iets als Q 27–28!,
which corresponds to Lk 11, 27–28) zelf zijn omlijstende verwantenperikoop
geconstrueerd heeft, een soort tegenhanger van Mc. 6, 1–6" (249). Crossan
J. D., 'Mark,' 98: "Mark received from his sources III 22b, 24–27 and III
31–34 in close relationship; he also received but separately a version of III
28–29a close to the Q text of that logion . . . The final redactional touch
(by Mk) was the creation of III 35 so that the relatives of Jesus with whom
Mark is interested are: mother, brothers, and sisters."
[47] Lambrecht J, 'Ware Verwantschap,' 247: besides other details, "in
hetzelfde vers (both in 3: 5 and 6: 3) is er sprake van zijn (Jesus') moeder,
broeders en zusters! . . . Men krijgt de indruk dat Marcus wellicht enkele
gegevens (. . .) uit hfd. 6 anticipeerede" in 3, 31–35.

the narrative of Mk himself (3, 31–34) as well as of Mt 12, 46–49, and the textual evidence of Mk 3, 32 concur to show that the concept "sisters" is foreign to the story. Still, this concept is introduced in v. 35. The evangelist goes now beyond the terms of the episode—but he does so in the precise terms of 6, 3: brothers, sisters, mother. The evangelist puts on Jesus' lips this time, all the degrees of relationships that the evangelist ascribes to Jesus in 6, 3—all these degrees, but no more than these.

In fact, the absence of any reference to "my father" in the sentence "this is my brother and sister and mother" (3, 35) is as conspicuous and deliberate here as the absence of Joseph in 6, 3. And there can be little doubt that the omission is based on the same grounds in both passages, namely: the evangelist's conviction that no man could be really called father of Jesus.[48]

Another observation confirms this conclusion. In Mk 10, 29 the evangelist refers to those who for Christ and the Gospel give up "brothers, sisters, mother, *father,* children, fields." It is striking that in this passage the order in relatives is exactly the same of our verse 35 (brother, sister, mother)—which verse, however, reverses the order of the episode to which it is attached ("his mother and brothers"). But, whereas 10, 29 goes beyond "mother" to include "father and children,"[49] our text in v. 35 ends with the mention of the mother, conspicuously excluding *"father* and children."[50] The passage in 10, 29 also shows that a more or less complete list of relatives is a literary cliché

[48] Concerning the brothers and sisters of Jesus the remark of McArthur H., 'Son of Mary,' seems to be pertinent: "The reference to the brothers and sisters of Jesus as if they were on a par with him is strange if the passage (Mk 6: 3) is implying that Jesus was illegitimate but his brothers and sisters legitimate. Or was it assumed that all the children were illegitimate? Surely this leads to absurdity!"

[49] Oddly enough, Mk 10, 30, which literally repeats v. 29, omits 'father.' No explanation can be offered for this omission. The phrasing of v. 29 stands, though.

[50] Crossan J. D., 'Mark,' 98: Mark "removed the following *patéra* from the sequence. That this is somewhat unusual is clear from the synoptic parallels: Mt IX (read XIX) 29 reorders the list into the expected order."

or form to indicate the *closest* (and dearest) attachments. This can be abundantly proved by texts like Mk 13, 12; Mt 10, 35–37; 19, 29, etc. It is a biblical "form" (Mk 7, 10ff; 10, 7; Mich 7, 6). Among the closest relatives the *father* is mentioned regularly, as the references given show. The omission of the father in Mk 3, 35 is an exception to the rule, it is against the natural expanse of the formula. The formula was deliberately shortened by the evangelist.

The state of affairs in Mk, therefore, is as follows. Mark does not even hint at any human father of Jesus; Mary appears as "mother" (of Jesus), but nothing is said about her husband or about her marital status; Joseph's name itself is *de facto* ignored by Mk, and there are unequivocal indications of a deliberate purpose of the evangelist to erase this name, or any mention of a human paternity for Jesus, from his Gospel; on the other hand, the evangelist is very emphatic in relating God and Jesus as "father" and "son." These details find a suitable explanation only if the evangelist is aware and convinced that Jesus had a human mother and a non-human father (but no human father).

If it is contended that Mk did not know of Jesus' virginal conception, the historical evidence from Mk *imposes* the only other alternative, namely: that Mk and his community had to *reject* any relationship of origin between Jesus and Joseph (6, 3) or between Jesus and any human father (3, 35).[51] In this

---

[51] Cfr Stauffer E., 'Jeschu Ben Mirjam,' 128: "Jesus was the son of Mary, not of Joseph. This is the historical fact. The Jewish polemic about Mary has interpreted this reality pornographically. The Christian Church has explained it in terms of parthenogenesis." Concerning this, McArthur H., 'Son of Mary,' 53, asks: "How is it plausible that the Evangelist (Mk) repeated the phrase—with its implications—without providing any hint in this gospel as to how the charge should be met?" If one contends that Mk was unaware of the implications, "this comes perilously close to conceding that there was no generally recognized custom of identifying an illegitimate son by his mother's name." Interestingly enough, the many quotations adduced by Stauffer (pps. 122f, 126ff) from various origins, either mention no father of Jesus or mention someone *other* than Joseph—never is Joseph said to be such a father. On the other hand, in some of the sources John the Baptist appears as "the son of Zachariah."

perspective the mention of God as father of Jesus could serve only the purpose of hiding a distasteful realization. But in no way does this evidence allow anyone to conclude that Joseph was Jesus' father or that Jesus had any (human) father.

Concerning the fourth Gospel, Brown's view is that "Overall, the scales tip in favor of Johannine ignorance of the virginal conception; and that means the ignorance of it in a late-first-century Christian community that had access to an early tradition about Jesus."[52] Fitzmyer agrees: "The Johannine Gospel obviously does not deny the virginal conception of Jesus, but it does not affirm it either . . . the Johannine Gospel can still refer to Him (Christ) as "the son of Joseph" and can remain silent about His virginal conception."[53]

Bethlehem, The Village of David

It is the conviction and the faith of the fourth evangelist that Jesus is "the Messiah." It is in this faith that he wrote his work (20, 21); it is this that Christ Himself confirms to the Samaritan woman (4, 25; cfr 10, 24f). The admission of Christ in 9, 37 (cfr 12, 34) amounts to the same thing. Furthermore, the admissions of Andrew (1, 42; cfr v. 45) and Martha (11, 27) no doubt express the evangelist's view. See 3, 28f; also 6, 69. It is against this faith of the evangelist that the comments of the crowds in 7, 42 have to be projected; some contended that Jesus could not be the Messiah because he was from Galilee: "Did not the Scripture say that the Messiah comes from the seed of David, and from Bethlehem, the village where David lived?"

The statement is placed on the lips of the crowd. In fact, however, it expresses the conviction of the evangelist and of his community, since for them Jesus was certainly the Messiah, and they know that the Scriptures (2 Sam 7, 12; Mich 5, 1; Ps 89, 4f) were fulfilled in Him. In Apc—a book of the same Johannine school—Christ, the key of David (3, 7; reference to Is 3,

[52] Brown R., 'The Virginal Conception,' 59.
[53] Fitzmyer J. A., 'The Virginal Conception,' 560.

7), is the scion from David (5, 5; reference to Is 11, 10.1; cfr Rom 15, 12), is the scion and the race of David (22, 16). If the evangelist makes the Jews say that Jesus is from Galilee, it is just to stress that they know nothing about Christ's mystery (see v. 52). This is the same literary and dialectic device used by the evangelist in 12, 34, where the evangelist certainly knows that Jesus is the Messiah, that He is going to die (v. 33) and that He "remains for ever"—though he has the crowds use the same concepts to express a different opinion; the device remains fundamentally the same when Caiphas, meaning something different, expresses the views of the evangelist, as he himself explains this time (11, 50ff; cfr 4, 12; 8, 57f).

This peculiar dialectic device should be emphasized, because it shows that, in spite of appearances, in Jn 7, 42 the evangelist does say that Jesus is not a native of Galilee but of Bethlehem, "the village where David lived," and that Jesus is of Davidic descent.

In the same direction another detail is to be emphasized. The place where the Messiah was to be born is not only Bethlehem, but it is also "the village where David lived"—this is the particular definition or description of Bethlehem that John gives. Such a description of Bethlehem has a lot in common with Lk 2, 4.11, in the infancy narratives: Joseph went to Judah, "to the city of David, which is called Bethlehem"; according to the angel, "Christ the Lord was born in the city of David." This similarity is not just a coincidence and, therefore, it is not irrelevant.

In the entire Jewish pre-Christian tradition Bethlehem is *never* described as "the city (or village) of David." For the Old Testament the "city of David" is not Bethlehem but Sion. The passage of 2 Sam 5, 9 records that David renamed Sion and called it the "city of David," and this was the biblical name of Sion for a long time to come, as can be seen in 2 Sam 5, 7; 6, 10.12.16; 1 Kings 2, 10; 3, 1; 4, 34 (3, 1), etc. This was still the name of the place long after David (2 Chron 21, 1.20; 27,

9; etc). The situation with Bethlehem, however, is completely different. The Bethlehem in Judah (there was another Bethlehem in Zabulon, Josh 19, 15; cfr Jud 12, 8.10) was called just Bethlehem, without any addition or explanation (Gen 35, 19; 48, 7; Ruth 1, 19.22; 2, 4; 4, 11 [but see 1, 1.2]; 1 Sam 16, 4; 17, 15, etc). But when the name of Bethlehem has to be further specified for whatever reason,[54] the technical and only form is "Bethlehem of Judah" (*Bethlehem yehudah*), which is used many times (Jud 17, 7.8.9; 19, 1.2.18 [twice]; Ruth 1, 1.2; 1 Sam 17, 12; the passage of Mich 5, 1 refers to "Bethlehem Ephrathah", cfr Gen 35, 19; 48, 7). Importantly, it is in accordance with this biblical usage that Mt refers to Bethlehem in the infancy narratives: Bethlehem of Judah (2, 1.5), Bethlehem land of Judah (2, 6). So far there is nothing like "Bethlehem the city (or village) of David."[55]

The usage of Luke and John in defining or describing Bethlehem as David's home-place is new and unusual. That is why the apparent coincidence is all the more striking. The case of Lk 2, 11 where "the city of David" is not explained by the addition "Bethlehem" shows that the expression has something of *formelhaft* to it.[56] This is true of 2, 4 also, when one realizes that it is not the "city of David" that describes Bethlehem, but it is Bethlehem that gives its identity to the city of David; Joseph came to "the city of David which is called Bethlehem."

[54] Aharoni Yohanan, *The Land of the Bible* (London, 2d reprint, 1968) 266: "When a town bears a very common name, the addition of a second element for the sake of clarity is not at all unusual. Thus a place name may be defined more precisely by the indication of its region, territory, or population . . . e.g. Bethlehem-Judah." This does not interfere with our argument.

[55] 1 Sam 20: 6 does say that David went to "his" city, i.e. Bethlehem, in the way that one goes to "his" home-town. No further implications. On the authority of Strack H.-Billerbeck P., *Kommentar zum NT*, I (München, 1922) 76, "Das judäische Bethlehem wird, abgesehen von den Zitaten aus dem AT, in der rabbin. Literatur nur sehr selten erwähnt." On p. 83 a rabbinic text reads "Bethlehem of Judah."

[56] Notice that both in 2, 4 and v. 5 *pólis David* is without article, as the very name of a place in perfect agreement with the Hebrew expression *c̄ir Dāwid*.

These remarks show that the expression in Jn 7, 42 "Bethlehem the village where David lived" is evidence of a Christian language,[57] even though it is ascribed to a Jewish crowd; it is the language of the evangelist who discloses his own convictions. This is all the more so that it is nearly unthinkable that a Jewish crowd would speak of the "village" of David. The remarks show, furthermore, that there is a significant coincidence between Jn and Lk—a coincidence which is based on this Christian way of describing Bethlehem by some sort of Christian messianic "formula." Significantly enough, in the entire New Testament (in the entire Bible, for that matter) this sort of formula is found only in Luke and in John. The contacts between Luke and John have been pointed out long ago.[58] In Luke, however, this formula is restricted to the infancy narratives, as is the name of Bethlehem itself not only in Lk but also in Mt. It is also in these narratives that the connection of Christ with David's lineage is particularly stressed. As for John, our passage in his Gospel where he refers to the origin of the Messiah from David to His birth in Bethlehem and to the fact that Bethlehem is "the village where David lived" contains different elements which are found in the infancy narratives.

The foregoing details can hardly be explained but on the basis that John was aware of the Christian belief that Jesus as

[57] Which is confirmed by the remark of Barrett C. K., *The Gospel according to St. John* (London, 1955) 273 about the reference to Mich 5: 2: "The use of this passage seems to be Christian," since it is mentioned in the rabbinic literature at a very late date. So also Brown R., *The Gospel according to John* (Anchor Bible, 29), (Garden City, 1966) 330: "On the basis of the parallelism between (v.) 27 and 42, then, we believe that the evangelist knew perfectly well of the tradition that Jesus was born in Bethlehem. Since he expected that this tradition would be known by his readers, the mistake of the Jews in (v.) 42 would be apparent to them, even as was the mistake in 27."

[58] Cfr Brown R., *ibid.*, XLVIf: ". . . it is with the peculiarly Lucan material that John has the important parallels . . . Some of the parallels may best be explained by assuming that the independent tradition behind John had features also found in the peculiar Lucan sources . . . such cross-influence . . . may well have taken place at an oral stage in the history of Gospel composition."

Messiah was in fact born in Bethlehem, the village of David—and from Davidic descent. The acquaintance of John with the infancy traditions is not easily dismissed.[59] The Johannine theology in Apc insists on the connections between Jesus—the Messiah—and David.

One more detail seems to confirm John's acquaintance with the infancy narratives. In 4, 44, as Jesus arrives precisely in Galilee, fleeing from Judah where he was persecuted (4, 1–3), John has Jesus say "that a prophet is not held in honor in his own (*idios*) home-land."[60] The text makes it abundantly clear that, in John's view, Galilee is not Christ's homeland—in spite of the fact that for those in Galilee (who are Christ's followers: 1, 45f) and for those in Judah (who are His enemies: 18, 5.7) as well as for the official opinion in Jerusalem (19, 19) Jesus is "from Nazareth" or is "the Nazarene," or is from Galilee in general (7, 42.52). Notice that in all these passages it is the people, not the evangelist, who say so. Conversely, the saying in 4, 44 which certainly harks back to 4, 1–3 (cfr 3, 22ff),[61] is evidence that in John's view Judah is Jesus' homeland—in spite of the fact that the evangelist knows that Jesus' "brothers" lived in Galilee (2, 12; 7, 3ff), that several of His disciples are

[59] Barrett C. K., *The Gospel,* 273: "We may feel confident that John was aware of the tradition that Jesus was born at Bethlehem (. . .) he writes here in his customary ironical style. The critics of Jesus ignorantly suppose that because he was brought up in Galilee he was also born there." Cfr Knoch Otto, 'Die Botschaft des Matthäus—evangeliums über Empfängnis und Geburt Jesu vor den Hintergrund der Christusverkündigung des Neuen Testaments,' *Zum Thema Jungfrauengeburt,* 55.

[60] This logion also is preserved by the synoptic tradition (Lk 4: 24 parall.) and, in a form very close to Lk, by Papyrus Oxyrhyncus 1, 5, which is now regarded as non-original (cfr Bajard J., 'La péricope de Nazareth,' 170 fnt 22; Segbroeck F., 'Jésus rejeté' 187 fnt 2) and in the Gospel of Thomas, 31.

[61] Cfr Dodd C. H., *Historical Tradition,* 237–238, 240. Bultmann R. K., *The Gospel of John,* (English trans. by G. R. Beasley-Murray, W. N. Hoare, J. K. Riches) (Philadelphia, 1971) 204, refers the logion to the people of Galilee. Schnackenburg Rudolf, *The Gospel According to St John* (English trans. by Smyth K.) (New York, 1965) 463, agrees. This is difficult not only on account of v. 45, but also because of the reference to 4: 1–3, besides the difficulties raised by Willensen J., 'La Patrie de Jésus selon Saint Jean,' *NTS* 11 (1961/2) 352f.

from Galilee (1, 43f.47; 12, 21; cfr 21, 1f), and that Jesus Himself "goes up to Jerusalem" as a pilgrim for the feasts (2, 13 [cfr 4, 45]; 5, 1; 7, 10). The impression is that, also in John's view, Jesus lives in Galilee, even if His ministry takes place in Jerusalem.

In spite of all external evidence, however, John maintains that Jesus' homeland is not Galilee but Judah. There is no reason why this term "home-land" (*patris*) should not express what is the most obvious alternative (cfr Mk 6, 4 parall.), namely, the place where one is—or is supposed to have been— born. Other explanations of Jn 4, 44 are too sophisticated to be convincing.[62] As a result, this passage shows that John knew that Jesus, though living in Galilee and supposed to be from Galilee, was, in fact, born somewhere in Judah[63]—i.e. in Bethlehem (7, 42). Once again, John appears to be acquainted with the traditions about Jesus' birth, traditions reported in the infancy narratives (Mt and Lk) only.

Mary, The Only Human Parent

As the evangelist knows that Jesus was born in Bethlehem, he also knows that he has a mother—but no father, except God. Obviously, this evangelist mentions twice a reference to Joseph as father of Jesus: Philip tells Nathanael that he has found the Messiah, "Jesus son-of-Joseph from Nazareth" (1, 45); the Jewish audience in the synagogue of Capharnaum reacts against Jesus' statement that he came down from heaven and asks "is this (man) not Jesus son-of-Joseph, whose father and mother we know?" (6, 42). But it is highly important to realize that both statements express the views of the people—which do not necessarily agree with the views of the evangelist. He certainly disagrees with the people in 6, 31ff.42ff; 7, 15; 8, 33.42.48.57; 9, 40; 12, 34, etc. We have already seen that in presenting Jesus as ben-Joseph (6, 42) John agrees with Lk and Mt who,

[62] Cfr Willemse J., 'La Patrie de Jésus,' 158–166.
[63] Dodd C. H., *ibid.*

independently of, and against, Mk, report that in the popular opinion Jesus was son of Joseph, though they knew this was not so, according to their own infancy narratives. The implication is that John's "quotation" of the popular view may be just that: a quotation.

It is to be noticed that both in Jn and in Lk the description of Jesus as "son-of-Joseph" is but Jesus' family name, it is his official identity as "ben-Joseph." Though such an identity usually implied biological connections, in itself the official identity or family name—ben-Joseph—does not stress such connections but rather social and juridical bonds (between Joseph and Jesus). It cannot be said, therefore, that the expression of the crowds precisely indicates biological connections: it is but the official identity of Jesus, the way in which the identity of that man could be expressed. Were Jesus an adoptive (or in any way legal) son of Joseph and were this known by the people, Jesus' official identity would be the same: "Jesus ben-Joseph"; still this identity would by no means denote biological origin (cfr Deut 24: 5–9; Ruth 4: 5–17).

In 6, 42, furthermore, we probably have to deal with the evangelist's peculiar dialectic device pointed out before. The misunderstanding of the situation shown by the unbelieving Jews is a means for the evangelist to teach the true mystery of Jesus. The reaction of the Jews was prompted by Jesus' statement that He "came down from heaven" (v. 41 and 42): the mention of Jesus' father and mother in this framework shows that the evangelist understands that statement in the sense of origin proper. In His answer to the Jewish question Jesus brings into sharp relief the notion of "the Father" (v. 44)—a Father whom no one has ever seen "except he who is from God: this one has seen the Father" (v. 45). This statement expresses the same thought of 1, 18 when Jesus, the incarnate Logos, is described by the evangelist as the "only begotten God[64] who is in the bosom of the Father." In the same context (1, 14) the

[64] The text is not uniform, but it certainly refers to the incarnate Logos.

incarnate Logos—who is identical with Jesus Christ, v. 17—is seen by the evangelist full of "glory as of an only begotten son from the Father" which He is. In this connection the entire context of the prologue is highly suggestive.

Still the popular opinion about Jesus as a "ben-Joseph" has some importance because it points to a social situation where Jesus could be taken for the son of two consorts, i.e., it points to a marital situation of Joseph and Mary. Incidentally, this is the same situation one finds in Mt and Lk, particularly in their infancy narratives—but not in Mk.

Over against this opinion of the people, which he does not ratify, the evangelist himself throughout his Gospel refers only to "the mother of Jesus" (2, 2.3), to "his mother" (2, 5.12; 19, 25), to "the mother" (19, 26). That the evangelist refers to Jesus' mother because he has a widowed mother in mind is not tenable, since one realizes that, in the same retrospective view, John knows that someone could mention Joseph as Jesus' father and (presumably) as Mary's husband (6, 42; 1, 45)—and he could do the same thing, were this his conviction.

On the other hand, it is striking that John does not even record the name of Mary (Jesus' mother), in spite of the fact that he names several other Marys by their names (11, 1.2.19 etc.; 12, 3; 19, 25; 20, 1, etc.)—he refers to her merely as "the mother of Jesus," etc. At the turn of the first century in the Christian tradition represented by the fourth Gospel the memory of "the mother of Jesus" survived, but no memory of Joseph as his father, which would be rather strange if the conviction was held that Joseph was in fact his father (cfr 6, 42 for the popular opinion). This is all the more so when one takes notice that the very first time that reference is made to Mary she is not introduced to the reader nor is she indicated by her name (cfr the contrast in 19, 25 and 11, 1f)—she is referred to as the mother of Jesus, which has a certain scent of tradition (cfr Acts 1, 14); this is how the Christian tradition referred to Jesus' origins. Even in the Johannine tradition Peter's descent is recorded as "Simon son of John" (1, 42; 21, 15–17) by the author himself; and the same thing applies to "Simon the Simon Iscariotes" (6, 71; 13, 26; cfr 13, 2 variant reading); in 21, 2 the Johannine tradition refers to "those of the Zebedee." None of the personages in the fourth Gospel is related to his/her mother—except Jesus, for whom no human father is indicated by the evangelist; the closest human father of Jesus is David (7, 42), according to the evangelist. The only other earthly relationship by which this evangelist identifies Jesus is the town Nazareth: He is "Jesus the Nazarene" (18, 5.7; 19, 19), which means "Jesus . . . from Nazareth" (1, 46). On the other hand, it is worth noticing that John does know of several "brothers" (plural) of Jesus (2, 12; 7, 3.6.10; cfr 20, 17)—but oddly enough, there is no evidence that he knows of any human father of Jesus.

It is this background that puts in the proper perspective another prominent element in John's Gospel: the insistent emphasis with which this gospel calls God Jesus' father, with all the depth of the Johannine Christology or Theology. This is an obvious fact, no proofs are needed. Only a few details could be pointed out. When in 1, 14 the evangelist refers to the incarnation of the Logos who from the beginning was with God and "was God" (divine) Himself (v. 1), through whom the entire creation came into being and whose glory was seen among us (1, 14; cfr 1 Jn 1, 1), the evangelist understands this Logos —who in v. 17 becomes Jesus Christ—as a *monogenes para patros,* as an only begotten son (coming) from a father. Whatever the value of *monogenes* in other places, the relationship son-father established in this text shows that such correlatives are to be taken in their proper sense. The different concepts in this passage, furthermore, are illustrated by 17, 4.24 where Christ asks the "Father" to give Him back the "glory" that he had—as a "gift" of the Father—"with you before the world existed." In the same context (v. 1) Christ understands Himself as God's son: glorify "your son."

Now in 1, 14 no human father is mentioned when the Logos "becomes man to dwell among us": only God appears as the Father of this only begotten Son who happens to be Jesus Christ (1, 17), who continues to be "in the bosom of the Father" (v. 18). Obviously, these passages just quoted show that the evangelist knew of a certain pre-existence of Christ—which becomes all the more apparent when John has Christ Himself say that "before Abraham come to be, I am" (8, 58). Significantly, in 8, 56 Jesus refers to Abraham as "your" (not "our") father (cfr v. 33.39.58). Importantly, Jesus stresses that He existed long before Abraham in the same context where He specifies that His Father is the God the Jews worship (8, 54). This claim is understood by the Jews—who in this case express John's views— literally: Christ "being a man makes himself God" (10, 33); and Christ maintains His claim (v. 36). The same thought is expressed in 5, 18 even more emphatically perhaps, in a comment of the evangelist himself: Jesus' claim "that he called God his own (*idios*) father" is understood in the sense that "he makes himself equal to God" (cfr 19, 7). In this context, v. 26 is highly suggestive: having life by Himself, the Father gave to the Son the gift of having life by Himself also.

The Johannine theology certainly understands that there is an element in the "incarnate" Logos dwelling among us that cannot derive from any human father. Whether one and the same "person" can have two fathers is not my problem now, though I find it difficult to accept.[65] If this theology is mentioned here, it is to bring into strong relief a definite purpose of the fourth evangelist: he knows and stresses that Jesus has a mother who is a woman, and a father who is not a man but God—Joseph is not mentioned in this fatherly role by the evangelist himself. This is all the more striking that most of the time it is Jesus Himself who calls God His father, in the strong sense we have seen.

[65] This is the reason suggested by Tertullian, *Adv. Marc.* 4, 10, why a virginal conception was needed in the case of Jesus, Son of God.

In this connection another detail is interesting. It seems that there is some reference in the fourth Gospel to the old insult that Christ was a bastard. It is in this sense that Jn 8, 41 has been understood since very early times,[66] where the Jews in an argument with Christ retort: "we are not born of fornication"— they are not bastards. This statement comes after a probably ironic question of the Jews in the same chapter (v. 19): "Where is your father?" The question of Philip in 14, 8 is considerably different. See also 8, 25: "Who are you?" In the same context of chapter 8 Christ complains that He honors his father, "but you insult me" (8, 49); it is later in the chapter (v. 54.58) that he discloses that His father is the God of the Jewish worship, and that He "was" before Abraham came to be. There is more. In 9, 29 the Pharisees know that God spoke to Moses "but this (Jesus), we do not know where he comes from." The expression can hardly indicate geographical origin; this could be easily found out—besides the fact that in the fourth Gospel everybody knows that Jesus is from Galilee (7, 42.52). Such a sentence can normally refer to one's origins.[67]

If these expressions of the evangelist do refer to the slander of illegitimacy, an important implication is that the evangelist could not avoid facing and considering the problem of Christ's origins. The implication is that the perspective that he offers concerning this point is all the more weighty and deliberate: for him Jesus has a mother (who is Mary) and a father who is God—but not Joseph. Even if those expressions are not meant as insults, they show that the evangelist did think of Christ's

[66] Cyril of Alexandria, *In Ioannem* 5, 551 (PG 73, 881f); Zigabenus Euthymius, *In Ioannem, in loc.* (8, 41) (PG 129, 1297).

[67] In 2 Sam 1: 13 the answer to "where are you from?" is "I am *the son* of an Amalekite"; in Tob 5: 5 (S); 7: 3 the answer to the same question is respectively "from the children of Israel," "from the children of Nephtali captives in Ninive." Cfr 1 Sam 25: 11; 30: 13 (LXX; Hebr "to whom do you belong?"); Jonas 1: 8. Ardnt-Gingrich note that such an expression indicates origin: "born of whom?", and understand that Jn 7: 27 could mean "of what kind of parents he was born" (but cfr Strack H.-Billerbeck P., *Kommentar zum NT*, II, 489). Liddle-Scott, *Greek-English Lexicon* 1, 2 also note that the sentence means origin.

origins; this is further stressed by the emphasis the same author places on the fact that Jesus Christ came "in the flesh"[68] (1 Jn 4, 2; 2 Jn 7) and "came through blood" (1 Jn 5, 6). And then the conclusion is the same: the perspective of the Johannine literature in this regard is not casual or unintentional. After all, the fourth Gospel was written long after Mt and Lk. If these came to know about the belief of the virgin birth, nothing precludes the possibility for the fourth evangelist to have become acquainted with it; this belief was held by the Johannine churches when Ignatius went through that area on his way to Rome (see below) about that time.

Perspectives in Other Johannine Writings

Beyond the fourth Gospel, I would like to touch upon some other details in the Johannine literature which are not even mentioned by either Brown or Fitzmyer. These details may not be decisive, but the perspective they offer certainly is a postively open possibility in our subject, one which cannot be lightly dismissed or ignored.

In 1 Jn 5, 18 the author says that "everyone who has been begotten of God (*ho gegennemenos ek tou theou*) does not sin; on the contrary he who was begotten of God, protects him (*all' ho gennetheis ek tou theou terei auton*) and the evil one does not touch him." The point for our subject is this: who is *ho gennetheis* (*aor.*) of God who guards him who does not sin? Certainly, there are other translations philologically possible,[69] but they were devised to go around the doctrine involved in the most obvious understanding of the text which is expressed in the translation above. In fact, it is the preference of many

---

[68] In 2 Jn 7 the present participle is used, not the perfect participle as in 1 Jn 4: 2. Surprising as it is, "in no way can this be a reference to the Christ of the Parousia," Schnackenburg R., *Die Johannesbriefe*, (Herders theologischer Kommentar zum NT 13/3) (Freiburg, 1963) 312f.

[69] Three other alternative translations: he who was begotten of God (*casus pendens*)—him (God) guards; he who was (once) begotten of God holds fast to him (God); he who was begotten by God guards himself.

authorities;[70] and Schnackenburg himself, who follows another opinion, has this to say about it: "The explanation preferred in more recent times understands *ho gennetheis* in reference to Christ. The following seems to speak for this view: a) it avoids the tension between *pas ho gegennemenos* and *ho gennetheis;* b) the uniformity in understanding the personal pronouns *auton* 18b and *autou* 18c of the Christian; c) the antithesis of this "begotten of God" (Christ) to the "evil one" (18c); d) the comparison with Jn 17, 12 and Apc 3, 10." These reasons seem to provide a very strong support for such an understanding. At any rate, this understanding is not only as good as all other translations, but it is even better, and it certainly is the most obvious.[71]

Since the possibility of referring *ho gennetheis ek tou theou* to Christ is very real, one cannot help comparing John's formula with that in Mt 1, 20 where Mary's child is characterized as *gennethen ek pneumatos* (begotten of the Spirit), which, in its turn, points to the action of the *pneuma* in Mary as a reason why *to gennomenon* (what is being begotten) will be called "Son of God" (Lk 1, 35). That the formula *ek tou theou* is interchangeable with *ek pneumatos* in the Johannine literature is obvious when one compares Jn 1, 13 with 3, 5.6.8.

It is true that the expression *gennasthai ek tou theou* (to be begotten of God) is used by John to denote the divine sonship of Christians also.[72] But, on the assumption that 1 Jn 5, 18b refers to Christ, the "generation" from God certainly implies more than the same notion when it applies to a Christian:

---

[70] Which can be seen in Schnackenburg R., *Die Johannesbriefe,* 281, fnt 1.
[71] *Id., ibid.,* notes that the main objection against this understanding is that Christ "is nowhere else characterized in this manner and he can hardly be so characterized in this context (why not 'the son of God' as in v. 20?)." Obviously this is not a strong objection. Variation or uniformity in formulas depend more on the mood of the writer than on any rigid rule. Nowhere else in the Johannine literature (or the entire New Testament) is Christ characterized as "the genuine God" except in our passage—which is "the peak of the Church's Christological confession," Schnackenburg R. *ibid.,* 291.
[72] By means of both perfect (Jn 3: 8; 1 Jn 2: 29, etc.) and aorist (Jn 1: 13).

in the same context, in v. 20 which continues the idea of v. 18, Jesus Christ (and precisely Jesus Christ) is said to be "the genuine God,"[73] and it is with this intensive meaning that Jesus Christ is characterized as *"the* Son (*hyos,* not *teknon*) of God" —which John does not say of any Christian. The term *hyos* never applies to Christians in the Johannine literature; it is used of Christ in His relationship to the Father, whereas Christians are characterized as *tekna* of God.

This understanding of the text is very possible and probable. Then, the literary and doctrinal connections with Mt 1, 20 and Lk 1, 35 receive all their weight and relevance. Furthermore, this understanding agrees perfectly with the general perspective of the fourth Gospel in regard to Jesus' origins. Now, this possibility, or even probability, remains open, as long as it is not proved wrong—which is not easily done; just to ignore the passage, however, is no alternative.

Other details regard the Apocalypse of John. Jesus is given divine attributes: the first and the last, the alpha and the omega, the beginning and the end (1, 17; 2, 8; 22, 13), the living one (1, 18), etc. But along with this, Jesus' human connections are stressed: He is "the lion of the tribe of Juda" (5, 5), He is "the root of David" (5, 5), He is "the root and the lineage of David" (22, 16). On the evidence of the fourth Gospel it is very likely that these human connections are no mere titles applied to Christ just because they are found in the Old Testament. They may well echo a factual conviction of the author in agreement with the infancy narratives in Mt and Lk. In a series of messianic titles (22, 16) Jesus also is characterized, in the third place, as "the bright morning star." This seems well to be another messianic title (whatever the understanding of 2, 28) which refers the reader to Num 24, 17. Then, a connection with the star theme in Mt 2 and the light theme in Lk 2, 32 (cfr 1, 18) is no absurdity.

[73] Cfr Schnackenburg R., *ibid.*

More important than this, but linked to it, is the narrative in Apc 12. Admittedly this is a difficult passage on account, first of all, of the literary form adopted by the writer in his book, and of his mental categories. Obviously, much is to be done yet to uncover the full meaning of this passage. But precisely because of this it should not be ignored in the present discussion. An important analysis of Apc 12 was made by Salgado;[74] this also is ignored altogether.

The woman of this chapter is not necessarily an abstract symbol. Both the Apocalypse and the Bible in general make symbols out of real persons or facts to characterize spiritual concepts or attitudes. Balaam and Balak characterize the Nicolaitans (2, 14); Jezabel characterizes the idolatrous attitude in the community (2, 20f); Sodom and Egypt characterize an obstinate and unfaithful Jerusalem doomed to destruction (11, 8); Babylon characterizes imperial Rome (16, 19; 18, 2, etc). Both Adam and Christ are concrete persons for Paul, but they are symbols of two types of mankind also (1 Cor 15, 45ff; Rom 5, 14ff). Cfr 2 Peter 2, 15; Jude 15. Thus, the woman in Apc can be Mary who is raised to the level of a symbol characterizing God's community in some of its particular aspects.

In fact, this woman "gave birth to a son, a male, who was to shepherd all the nations with an iron rod, and the child was caught up to God and to his throne" (5). The Dragon, however, stood before the woman about to give birth, ready to devour her child when it should be born (v. 4). That is why the woman "wailed in the pangs of childbirth (*odinousa*) as she

---

[74] Salgado Jean-Marie, 'Le chapitre XII de l'Apocalypse à la lumière des procedés de composition littéraires de Saint Jean,' *Maria in Sacra Scriptura* 5, 293–360, with abundant bibliographical footnotes. Cfr Kassing A. Th., *Die Kirche und Maria. Ihr Verhältnis im 12. Kapitel der Apokalypse* (Düsseldorf, 1958) 158ff; Feuillet André, 'Le Cantique des Cantiques et l'Apocalypse' *RechSR* 49 (1961) 345–353; Montagnini Felice, 'Le "signe" d'Apocalypse 12 à la lumière de la christologie du Nouveau Testament,' *NRT* 89 (1967) 414ff. For an unusually original idea cfr Pétrement S., 'Une suggestion de Simone Weil à propos d'Apocalypse XII,' *NTS* 11 (1964/5) 291–296, who maintains that the woman is the Holy Spirit.

labored to give birth" (v. 3). Obviously, the fortunes of the child reflect the fortunes of the Messiah, of Jesus. But, then, the relationship of his "birth" of the woman, and of his persecution by the Dragon, to the infancy narratives is to be explored —but not denied or ignored. Within the context of the child's "birth," of the anguish of his mother, and of the readiness of the Dragon to devour the child, both the persecution of the child by Herod (Mt 2, 13–22)—who "was searching for the child to do away with him"—and the prediction of Simeon to Mary (Lk 2, 34f) are highly suggestive. It is particularly so when all these details are placed within the general perspective of the New Testament, where the emphasis lies on the mother of Jesus, but not on a human father.

It should be insisted that it is not my purpose to build any solid evidence on these details in 1 Jn and in Apc. At the same time, an honest inquiry in the present discussion cannot ignore these passages before the possibilities they offer are convincingly precluded. This has not yet been done.

The general perspective of Paul, rather than some particular texts in isolation, is important. Obviously, in Phil 2, 6–7 Paul admits a certain pre-existence of Christ when Jesus existed "in the form of God"[75] and "was equal to God" (cfr Jn 5, 18), before he took on "the form of a slave."

No Mention of Joseph

This view is expressed by Paul at the time of the great epistles,[76] a period to which his epistle to the Galatians also belongs. It is this group of epistles, as a group, that is relevant here. As a matter of fact, when in 2 Cor 8, 9 Paul maintains that the Lord Jesus Christ "being rich became poor" in order to make us rich with His poverty, he certainly refers to the pre-existence of Christ in the form of God before His *kenosis* as He became a slave.[77] The same conviction is expressed in 1 Cor 10, 4: the rock following the Israelites in the desert was Christ Himself[78] (cfr Rom 10, 6 also).[79] This Pauline perspective puts in a particular light the characterization of Christ as "*the* Son of God" used very often by Paul in his epistles (Rom 1, 3; 8, 3.29.31; 1 Cor 1, 9; 15, 28; 2 Cor 1, 2f. 19; Gal 1, 13, etc.). Particularly emphatic seems to be the formula "his own (*idios*) Son" in Rom 8, 31 (cfr v. 29).

It is against this background of Christ's pre-existence and of His quality as "*the* Son of God" that an omission in Paul gains its appropriate relief: that Paul *never* mentions any human father of Jesus. Not only the name of Joseph is omitted alto-

---

[75] Cfr Spicq Ceslas 'Note sur morphé dans les papyrus et quelques inscriptions,' *RB* 80 (1973) 37–45.

[76] Cfr Schweizer E., 'Zur Herkunft,' 105–109.

[77] *Id., ibid.,* 108.

[78] *Id., ibid.,* 106f. Cullmann Oscar, *ThWNT* VI, 97: "The same Christ, acting in history, stands over both the old and the new covenant in His pre-existence and post-existence."

[79] Schweizer E., 'Zur Herkunft,' 107.

gether in Paul's writings, but also any human paternity of Christ is ignored by Paul, and on the basis of what follows we may say that it was unknown to him. That a semitically-minded person like Paul disregards the paternity of the man he is devoted to is rather strange, to say the least.

No one can say that Paul was not interested in Christ's human origins. In Rom 1, 3 Paul stresses Christ's origins "according to the flesh"—as over against his quality of "Son of God." In Rom 9, 5 he again manifests his interest in Christ's origins "according to the flesh." In formulas of this kind the expression "according to the flesh" certainly indicates blood ties and family relationships. Evidence for this are passages like Rom 4, 1; 9, 8; 11, 13 (cfr 11, 1; 1 Cor 10, 28; 2 Cor 11, 18.22; Phil 3, 3.5, etc.; cfr Rom 8, 3 also.) Still, in this particular regard Paul knows that Christ is descended from Israel (Rom 1, 3; 5, 12), from Abraham (Gal 3, 16; cfr Rom 4, 13), and from David (Rom 1, 3; 15, 12)—but he stops there; he does not mention any other father of Jesus "according to the flesh." In other cases related to Salvation History Paul stresses paternity very strongly: Abraham was the father of both Ismael and Isaac, in spite of the fact that the latter was born "according to the spirit" (Gal 4, 22.29; cfr Rom 9, 7; 4, 18f); Isaac was the father of Jacob and of Esau (Rom 9, 9ff).

But, when considered in its context, the expression "according to the flesh" in Rom 1, 3 and 9, 5 suggests other implications besides human nature. In the first case Paul refers to the Son of God born of the seed of David "according to the flesh." In the second, the reference is to the Israelites from whom Christ comes *to kata sarka,* as far as the flesh is concerned. The point is this: why should this remark be added? It is obvious that every merely human being is born "according to the flesh," and that is why it is not stressed in other similar cases, because no one stresses the obvious. In the case of Christ, however, His quality of "Son of God" and his pre-existence are very present to Paul's mind, and that is why he adds the remark mentioned.

The implication is that Christ had another origin *not* according to the flesh, *not* human.[80] This is all the more so for those who, like Brown,[81] admit that Rom 9, 5 should be read as follows: "The Israelites . . . from whom Christ comes as far as the flesh is concerned—he who is God over all things. . . ." But it is clear enough in Rom 1, 3: God's Son "who was born of David's seed according to the flesh."[82]

Born of a Woman

The mention of no human paternity of Christ, the emphasis on Christ's pre-existence, His quality of "Son of God," the remark that Christ had a birth according to the flesh with its implications, Paul's interest in Christ's human origins—all these details in the Pauline writings form the framework within which the passage in Gal 4, 4 has to be read. This is a passage

[80] Schweizer E., 'Röm. 1, 3f, und der Gegensatz von Fleisch und Geist vor und bei Paulus,' *Neotestamentica*, 189: "If the formula of Rom 1: 3f is interpreted, not in a strictly local sense as a description of the two spheres in which Christ is Lord, but rather in a modal sense as a description of both ways of being, in which he lives, if at the same time *sárx* and *pneûma* are referred to him individually—then his two 'Natures' are described; and this is only logical, even though in the Church doctrine a *Nacheinander* of both natures is turned into a *Miteinander*." See Rom 9: 5, however, where no opposition to the Spirit is mentioned and where, according to Schweizer himself (p. 181), Paul uses 'according to the flesh' "rein neutral für die menschliche Abstammung Jesus." See, furthermore, Schweizer E., *Das Evangelium nach Mk* 147: "Rom 1: 3f, therefore, represents something like *Zweistufenchristologie*. That a solution, however, in terms of a merely historical *Nacheinander* is not enough, was already felt by Paul when he placed the dignity title 'Son of God' in Rom 1, 3 before the quotation, thereby saying that Christ already is Son of God from eternity, so that he showed his divine sonship precisely in the lowliness of his earthly life and death (Gal 4, 4f, cfr 3, 13)."

[81] Brown R., *Jesus God and Man* (Milwaukee, 1967) 21f.

[82] Important chronological implications would result if one accepts the "formelhaft" character of Rom 1: 3–4, which seems to be fairly well established. Cfr Duling Dennis C., 'The Promises to David and their Entrance into Christianity—Nailing down a likely Hypothesis,' *NTS* 20 (1973) 72: "As far as I am aware, all current scholars of Paul believe that Rom. I 3–4 contains a very early formula . . . Most reconstructions would include 'according to the flesh' and 'according to the spirit of holiness,' as part of the original formula since the latter expression is documentable in Jewish texts and is not the typically Pauline form of flesh/spirit antithesis."

important to our discussion, and Mariology has not yet exploited it as it should. The passage is this: "As the fullness of time came, God sent out his son born of a woman, born under a law" (*exapesteilen ho theos ton hyion autou, genomenon ek gynaioks* . . .). The text continues in v. 6 in this way: "God sent out (*exapesteilen*) the Spirit of his Son into our hearts."

There can be no doubt that the birth of God's Son "of a woman" is the actual way in which the Son of God was born according to the flesh. It is striking that, in his interest in Christ's human origins, the *only* immediate link that Paul establishes between the "Son of God" and mankind is through a woman[83]—whereas he is ignorant of any human paternity. It is striking, furthermore, that when this immediate link is established by Paul, over against the human mother, it is God who appears as father of Christ; even though born of a woman, Christ is "*the* son of God." He has a human mother but a divine father, with no mention, here or elsewhere in Paul, of a human father. The two agents that Paul mentions in connection with Christ's birth according to the flesh are a woman and God.

This is all the more striking when one realizes Paul's perspective in other similar cases of Salvation History. Further down the same chapter 4 in Gal, Paul also mentions the mothers of Isaac and Ismael; but their partner in regard to their motherhood is Abraham. Even though Paul would say that Isaac is born "according to the spirit," he points out that he is son of Abraham and that the partner of Sara is Abraham—not God; nor is Isaac called son of God. The following parallelism is instructive:

[83] Cfr O'Connor Edward, 'The Virgin Mary in the perspective of Salvation History,' *Oikonomia* (Festschr. for O. Cullmann) (Hamburg, 1967) 277: ". . . it is Mary who directly and personally fulfills Israel office of engendering the Savior. Israel achieve its purpose through her . . . Thus, it is from Mary, ultimately, that the Savior comes forth to rule His people (Mich. 5: 2). It is through her that mankind is related to Jesus by that bond of flesh that is the basis of the Redemptive economy. Through her, mankind, and Israel in particular, are brought into conjunction with the saving humanity of Christ."

ho theos ton hyion autou (exapes-   *Abraam dyo hyious eschen . . .*
teilen) genomenos ek gynaikos   *ek tes paidiskes . . . ek tes eleu-*
                                         theras

The pre-eminence of the father (Abraham) is again stressed
in Rom 9, 7f and in 4, 16–19 where Sara is explicitly mentioned
also. Otherwise than in Gal 4, 21–31, these passages do not
deal with Christian freedom, but precisely with the "seed" of
blessing which is the child of Sara—but he is "seed of Abraham."

The same interest for the father is manifested by Paul in
Rom 9, 10–13 as he draws the line of Salvation History further.
Again, he mentions the mother of Jacob and Esau, Rebekah.
But she does not appear alone, she appears associated with her
husband, the father of her children. Paul's concern is all the
more obvious since the specification "Isaac our father" is an additional unnecessary clause. It may be added that in Paul's
argument at this point (God's gratuitous and free choice), the
mention of a father was not required—but he does mention the
father all the same.

It is against this background that the phrasing of Gal 4, 4
is striking.[84] Precisely when Paul reaches the goal and the end
of Salvation History at the "fullness of time" with "the seed
which is Christ" (Gal 3, 16f), he mentions only the mother of
the "seed"—and she is not associated with any man, she is associated only with God, and the son of the woman appears
precisely as "*the* Son of God."

There is more. Our passage of Gal 4, 4 is part of a development which starts with ch. 3. Now, in this chapter 3 the connections of Christ with Abraham are the only topic; and the
point of Paul is that the "seed" referred to in God's promise to
Abraham is not the entire progeny of Abraham: the Scripture

---

[84] A historical survey of the interpretations of this passage can be seen in
Roover Emile de, 'La maternité virginale de Marie dans l'interprétation de
Gal 4, 4,' *Studiorum Paulin. Congr. Intern. Cath.* (AnBib 18) 2 (Rome,
1963) 17–37.

"does not say 'and to your seeds' as referring to many, but 'and to your seed' who is Christ, as referring to only one" (v. 16). Sara is not even mentioned this time; only the father, Abraham, is the all important element. As Paul carries the line of the promise further in Rom 9, 10, he stresses that this line is drawn through the father, Isaac. The same thing is true in Rom 1, 3 where it is David who marks the line of God's "promise through his prophets." Now, when the promise comes to fulfillment and the "one seed" of Abraham comes into existence no man is there: the one intended "seed" is born of a woman—and she bears "the Son of God." This is an obvious departure from the Pauline— and biblical—patterns. Even the people of Nazareth character-ized Jesus as "son of Joseph." But Paul fails to do so.

Within the framework of Paul's thought some other elements in Gal 4, 4 acquire a particular significance in regard to the present discussion. For the idea of God "sending" His Son, the Greek term is *exapostéllein,* which we translated by "to send out." Rengstorf[85] rightly notes that usually there is no appreci-able difference between this Greek verb and *apostellein* (to send). And this is why he dismisses Zahn's contention that Jesus existed with God even before he was born of a woman. The same writer, however, notes also that both in John and in Paul the Christological content of the notion "to send" depends only "on the Christological context in which it is used"—and, we may add, on the particular writing habits of a particular author.

In the New Testament *exapostéllein* is used only by Luke (4 times in the Gospel; 7 times in Acts) and by Paul (twice). The use in Luke always indicates the notion of "sending out" of some place (cfr Lk 20, 10; 24, 49; Acts 9, 30; 11, 22; 12, 11; 17, 14, etc.), which is the connotation of the preposition *ek.* This verb is used by Paul only in our passage, Gal 4, 4.6. It seems that Paul perceives a distinction between the term under discussion and *apostellein,* which is used by Paul, according to

---

[85] Rengstorf K. H., *ThWNT* 1, 397f, 403.

the propriety of the Greek language,[86] when the *mission* or commission entrusted is emphasized (Rom 10, 15; 1 Cor 1, 17; 2 Cor 12, 17). Interestingly enough, the only other passage where Paul speaks about God "sending" his Son is Rom 8, 3— and this time he uses *pempein*.[87] Now, "in the NT in the use of *pempein* the emphasis falls upon the sending as such; in that of *apostellein,* upon the commission attached to the sending—according to whether the sender or the envoy are the predominant interest."[88] This is the true meaning of *exapostéllein*[89] in Gal 4, 4. In fact, Ardnt-Gingrich mention this passage of Gal 4, 4 in the entry of this verb in their dictionary, and understand that God, "sent out" his Son *ex ouranou,* from heaven; they refer to Ps 57, 3.

This meaning of the Greek term can hardly be questioned in our passage on account of its presence in 4, 6, the only other instance of this verb being used by Paul: "God *sent out* the Spirit of his Son into our hearts" (cfr Lk 24, 49). There can be little doubt that the Spirit is sent out not only because "his coming is God's act" but also because He is prior to His being sent, and comes from God or "from heaven"—which agrees with the meaning of *pempein* in Jn 14, 26; 15, 26; 16, 7.

This understanding of *exapostéllein* squares perfectly with the Pauline perspective about Christ's pre-existence, as pointed out above, with its implications concerning Christ's characterization as "the Son of God."[90] In point of fact, our text in Gal 4, 4. reflects the same conception as that of Phil 2, 6f and 2 Cor 8,

---

[86] *Ibid.,* 405f.

[87] Which, with the exception of Rom 8: 3 and 2 Thess 2: 11, Paul always applies (14 times, including 2 Cor 8: 18, 22 *sym-*) to his own envoys to the various communities.

[88] Rengstorf K. H., *op. c.* 403. As for Rom 8: 3, he notes (fnt 8) that "the emphasis may lie not so much on the sending out of Jesus as on his coming as God's act; so far, *pémpein* makes good sense here." But other considerations in the text above make the use of this verb perfectly normal.

[89] The primary meaning of *exapostéllein* is "to dispatch, to send forth": Liddle-Scott.

[90] Schweizer E., 'Zur Herkunft,' 108; In Gal 4: 4 Jesus' "pre-existence is not explicitly stated, but it is taken for granted as a matter of fact. The verb

9: when Christ is born of a woman He becomes "subject to law" (3, 13 says that He becomes "a curse" under the law), just as He becomes "poor" (2 Cor 8, 9) and "a slave" (Phil 2, 7); and He becomes "born of a woman" just as He "comes to exist in the likeness of man." He also is "sent out" of that situation in which, being the Son of God, He "was in the form of God" and "was rich." That is why the verb *exapostéllein* connotes Christ's pre-existence and His being sent out from some place, i.e. from heaven—not because of merely linguistic considerations but, first of all, because of the "Christological context in which it is used," namely Paul's Christological context and his use of Greek terms.[91]

This understanding puts the notion *genómenon ek gynaikos,* "born of a woman," in a particular light. Admittedly, besides other connotations, *ginesthai* also can be used to express biological origin proper. But, again, it is Paul's own use of language that is decisive. Now, Paul does not use *ginesthai* with genetic connotations one single time—this also is the case with the entire New Testament.[92] Still, this is the verb he uses in reference to the Son of God as He "comes to exist" according to the flesh from David's seed (Rom 1, 3) or "from a woman" (Gal 4, 4). This is all the more significant when one realizes that in other cases of Salvation History in the same passage of Gal 4 Paul uses *gennan* (to beget) in various forms precisely because in these cases he stresses the "genetic" connotations; and this is true not only of those "begotten" according to the flesh but also of those begotten "according to the Spirit"

---

exapostéllein used here is found in Paul in this place only and in the parallel sentence v. 6." He refers to Wisd 9: 10: "Send her (Wisdom) out from the holy heavens, and from the throne of your glory send (*pémpein*) her."

[91] Cfr Legault André, 'Saint Paul a-t-il parlé de la maternité virginale de Marie?' *Sciences Ecclésiastiques* 16 (1964) 487: "God sent forth his Son who, therefore, let it be emphasized, was manifestly preexisting with him."

[92] The only exception is a variant reading in Hebr 11: 12, which is not even mentioned in the recent critical edition of the NT by Kurt Alland and others.

(Gal 4, 23f.29). Both Ismael and Isaac were *gennethentes* (begotten) because "Abraham had two sons"; Jacob and Esau were likewise *genethentes* because Rebekah "conceived of one man, of Isaac our father" (Rom 9, 11). The accuracy in Paul's use of language and, therefore, the Apostle's thought can be better evaluated when one compares these two passages in the same chapter 4 of Gal:

(The Son of God) *genomenos* (came to exist) *ek gynaikos*[93] (Gal 4, 4)	(Abraham's children) *ho men ek tes paidiskes gegennetai* (was begotten or born), *ho de ek tes eleutheras* (Gal 4, 23)

Others are "begotten," but the Son of God, as He enters His life "according to the flesh," "comes into existence,"[94] (from the seed of David and through a woman)—just as He "comes to existence" subject to a law (Gal 4, 4), or in the likeness of man (Phil 2, 7). As the Son of God comes to exist according to the flesh, Paul's expression comes very close to John's: "the Word came to existence (*egeneto*) as flesh" (Jn 1, 14). Paul's use of language is in keeping with the rest of the New Testament, which applies *gennan* (to beget) to Christ only when God is the agent explicitly or implicitly (Mt 1, 16.20; Lk 1, 35; Acts 13, 33; Hebr 1, 5; 5, 5; 1 Jn 5, 18 see above; cfr Mt 2, 1.4; Jn 18, 37 where the passive is used with the meaning "to be born").

The picture which emerges from an analysis of Paul's letters agrees with the rest of the New Testament. Paul does not offer any evidence of a human paternity for Christ. He is very careful

---

[93] Cfr Mt 1: 16: "of whom (Mary) Jesus was begotten" (or born: *egennēthe*, passive, in agreement with 1: 20).

[94] Legault A., 'Saint Paul . . .' 488, supported by Lagrange, whom he quotes, maintains that in Gal 4: 4 Paul uses *genómenon* instead of *genetón* because "when speaking about the Incarnation Paul intentionally avoids the word *naissance* (being born) that might suggest the passing from non-being to being."

in choosing his terms when he refers to Christ's origins "according to the flesh" and, then, he departs from his own—and from general biblical—patterns so as to refrain from suggesting any human genetic intervention in Christ's coming into His existence according to the flesh. On the other hand, in agreement with the rest of the Christian tradition Paul knows of the "brothers of the Lord" (1 Cor 9, 4; Gal 1, 19)—and still, with the rest of the Christian tradition again, he knows of a mother of Jesus but of no human father.[95]

Other New Testament Writings (except Mt and Lk)

In the rest of the New Testament writings, except Mt and Lk, no mention is made of Mary or Joseph, of a mother or of a human father of Jesus, nor is there any reference to Jesus' brothers. In fact, very few elements relevant to our discussion are found in these writings.

In the pastoral epistles an important detail is that Jesus is characterized as "the great God and our savior Christ Jesus who gave himself for us" (Tit 2, 13; cfr 2 Tim 4, 1). The passage in 1 Tim 3, 16 certainly refers to a certain pre-existence of Christ "who appeared in flesh"[96] (cfr 1 Tim 1, 9f). 2 Tim 2, 8 stresses that Jesus Christ is "of David's seed," a traditional datum known ever since Rom 1, 3 and which is therefore, anterior to Paul. The Gospel traditions contain this information also, and not only in the infancy narratives.

In the epistle to the Hebrews the doctrine of Christ being God and Son of God is emphasized from the very outset (1, 2–9; 4, 14; 5, 5.8; 6, 6; 7, 28). Accordingly, the author refers very explicitly to Christ's pre-existence in 1, 10, and, particular-

---

[95] Concerning the silence of Paul and other writers of the NT in this matter, the remark of Nellessen Ernst, *Das Kind und seine Mutter. Struktur und Verkündigung des 2. Kapitels im Matthausevangelium,* (Stuttgarter Bibelstudien 39), (Stuttgart, 1969) 109, is quite pertinent: "An explicit discussion on the peculiar circumstances of Jesus' conception and birth is to be expected only where the beginning of Jesus' human life become the object of a narrative description."

[96] Cfr *Ad Diogn.* XI.

ly in 7, 16f when Christ is said to be a priest "by virtue of an indestructible life" in the manner of Melchizedech—who appearing "without father, without mother, without genealogy, having no beginning of lifetime nor end of life, *but being like the Son of God,* remains a priest forever" (7, 3). It is in this perspective that the "appearance" of Christ in 9, 26 obtains its proper meaning and dimension (cfr 13, 8 also).

Still, the author of Hebrews knows that Christ has human ties too. He knows that Christ, far from descending from Levi, "belonged to another tribe, none of whose members ever officiated at the altar. In fact it is clear (*prodelon*) that our Lord rose from the tribe of Judah, regarding which Moses said nothing about priests" (7, 13f). The author is familiar with the tradition which traces Jesus back to the tribe of Judah. This is not his private view or his particular information or deduction since "it is known to all"[97] that it is so—this was common knowledge at the time the letter was written, at least in the community of the addressees and in that of the sender.[98] This fact shows that the author is not drawing conclusions from any scriptural passage, for instance that Christ is "son of David," which is never stated in this epistle. Such possibility is further excluded by the realization that the contention is something new and contrary to the biblical legislation concerning priesthood. Christ's origin from Judah, therefore, is based on common knowledge. That this common knowledge was just a theological deduction from the Scriptures and was not based on real facts is yet to be proved. What cannot be denied is that on this point the tradition known to the author and community of Hebrews agrees perfectly with a fact which in the entire New Testa-

[97] Ardnt-Gingrich, under *pródēlos,* for Hebr 7: 14.

[98] Spicq C., *L'Epître aux Hébreux* (Paris, 1953) 190: "The author has recourse to the knowledge that his readers have of Jesus' historical life, and their faith. They know—on the evidence of the promises (. . .), of the facts and of the gospel documents—that 'Our Lord' . . . came forth from Juda."

ment is explicitly attested only in the infancy narratives of Mt and Lk, and implicitly in Jn only.

In order to complete the picture of the New Testament outside Mt and Lk, it can be added here that the book of Acts supports the general Christian tradition. The name of Joseph is not even mentioned. Any human father of Jesus is ignored altogether, i.e. Jesus is not related to any immediate human father, in spite of the fact that he is descended from David (2, 25ff; 13, 2f.34ff; cfr 15, 16) and possibly from Abraham (3, 25). In point of fact, far from being identified by His father, Jesus is identified as Jesus (Christ) "the Nazarene" (*Nazoraios*) (2, 22; 3, 6; 4, 10; 6, 14; 22, 8; 26, 9), and His followers are known as the "sect of the Nazarenes" (24, 5), apparently from the name of the town Nazareth as it explicitly stated in 10, 38; "Jesus of Nazareth."

On the other hand, the author does mention "Mary the mother of Jesus, and His brothers" (1, 14). It is true, this detail squares perfectly with the character of Lk's infancy narratives, but it does not necessarily reflect Lk's particular view. The group of "Mary His (Jesus') mother and His brothers" belongs to the common Gospel tradition (Mk 3, 31 parall.), and the actual formula in Acts 1, 14 is very close to the formula in Jn 2, 12 in connection with other passages of the Johannine tradition (2, 1ff; 7, 2.5.10; 19, 25f). To the Pauline tradition "the brothers of the Lord" are well-known (1 Cor 9, 5; Gal 1, 19); and Gal 4, 4 certainly refers to the mother of Jesus, even though her name is not mentioned. On the other hand, in his Gospel Luke refers to Joseph as the assumed father of Jesus (3, 23; 4, 22)—something he does not do in Acts 1, 14 nor in the entire book. In this, Acts agrees with the whole New Testament also.

A Summary

An analysis of the New Testament material leads to the results that can be summarized in the conclusions which follow. In the first place, the elements in the New Testament connected with our subject do *not* suggest or imply *any contradiction* with the infancy narratives in Mt and Lk. More in particular, concerning the question of Mary's virginal conception there is no conflict at all between the rest of the New Testament and the narratives in Mt and Lk in regard to a bodily virginal conception of Jesus.[99] This is a merely negative realization. But some other positive elements can be pointed out.

In fact, there are several agreements between the infancy narratives and the rest of the New Testament: Jesus appears as the Son of God; some kind of pre-existence is ascribed to Him; and that is why He comes into existence "according to the flesh"; Jesus' human origins are traced back to a "woman," to "his mother," *only;* as for His blood attachments, Jesus is not linked to any human father, to the point that, except for Mt, Lk and Jn (see next two paragraphs), the name of Joseph is not even mentioned—and this is precisely the case with Paul and Mk, among, others; Jesus is descended from David and from Abraham; Jesus is said to be a native of Judah, not of Galilee, whatever the popular views; He is "from Bethlehem the village where David lived," and not from Nazareth, in spite of the fact that He is often identified as the "Nazarene," which agrees, once more, with the infancy narratives. Cfr Apc 12.

There is more. In some cases it is only obvious that the writers phrased their statements very carefully in order to avoid any suggestion to the effect of linking Jesus to any human father. Mk 6, 3 is the clearest example because, against the entire

---

[99] This is how it is stated by Vawter Bruce, *This Man Jesus* (Garden City, 1973) 192: ". . . those New Testament sources that make nothing of a virgin birth of Jesus also say nothing to rule one out, even in a most literal and unavoidable sense."

Gospel tradition, as attested by Mt, Lk and Jn, he changes the wording of the people's amazement in order to make Jesus "son of Mary" instead of "son of Joseph," which is against the Jewish established usage also. It is in this light that Mk 3, 35 discloses its full significance, when Jesus refers to His "brother, sister and mother," but he falls short of mentioning "His father,"—as the usual formula would have required—as one of His human relatives. But the same careful phrasing can be noticed in Rom 1, 3 and Gal 4, 4 when Paul refers to Christ's birth "according to the flesh" as a coming into existence, but not as a "being begotten," as does in the cases of Isaac, Ismael, Jacob and Esau. This is true of Jn 1, 14 also, when the evangelist accurately notes that the Word "came into existence as flesh" (cfr 1 Jn 5, 18). The same tendency is perceptible in Gal 4, 4 where Paul refers to Christ's birth of a woman as a being "sent out" by God, as well as when only God appears as the counterpart of the woman as "the" Son of God is born of a woman—whereas any mention of a human consort is omitted, contrary to Paul's own custom.

Whereas throughout the New Testament the memory of the "mother" of Jesus survives and is carefully preserved associated with the name "Mary," the same thing cannot be said of a strictly fatherly role of Joseph. In a tradition rooted in Jewish thought and social and legal categories this sounds truly strange. On the other hand, the death of Joseph is neither reported nor referred to in the New Testament. All this silence would be surprising, were Joseph the real father of Jesus.

As a matter of fact, it is impossible to prove on the New Testament evidence that Joseph is the father of Jesus or that Jesus has a known, legitimate, human father. In the fourth Gospel the view of the evangelist himself is that Jesus has a mother (cfr Apc 12); he himself does not refer to any father of Jesus except God. He mentions the popular view which holds that Jesus is a "ben-Joseph" (son of Joseph). But the evangelist does not suggest in any way that he himself subscribes to such a view. His particular use of irony and misunderstanding in the audience as a literary device rather suggests that he does not subscribe to such an understanding. Mk, in his turn, ignores the name of Joseph altogether as well as any (human) paternity for Jesus. He introduces Jesus simply as "the son of Mary," who appears associated with "the brothers of Jesus" but not with any husband. Again, Paul, who admits some sort of pre-existence of Christ, knows that "the son of God" had a birth "according to the flesh." But he does not know of any father of Jesus more immediate than Abraham and David. Still, he knows that it was a "woman" who brought the Son of God into existence according to the flesh. Unlike Sara and Rebekah, however, this woman does not conceive of any man, she is not associated with any husband. The book of Acts does not know of Joseph or of any other human father of Jesus either; this book knows only of "Mary the mother of Jesus." Christ's mother or (human) father are not referred to in the rest of the New Testament—except in Mt and Lk. As a matter of fact, it is only Mt and Lk, as we shall see, who report that Mary, the mother of Jesus, lived in a marital situation at the time when Jesus was born (and conceived, we may confidently say); it is they who state that Joseph was Mary's husband. Oddly enough, they give this information precisely in the infancy narratives where they also deny right away that Joseph is the father of Jesus. In the rest of their respective Gospels both evangelists reflect the popular opinion about Jesus' father—but they report it as a popular opinion, not as their own conviction. In point of fact, Lk takes good care to point out that Jesus "was believed" to be Joseph's son. The picture, therefore, that emerges from the entire New Testament does not allow the conclusion that Jesus is the son of Joseph or of any legitimate human father.

Anyone who denies the virginal conception draws upon himself the burden of going in search of a father for Jesus and to give this father a name. Otherwise, if he is a Christian, he is faced with the odd situation of being a follower and a worshiper of a bastard. But finding a father for Jesus is no easy task, because the evidence of the NT positively discards Joseph, and other documents are not available.

The positive side of the foregoing remark is that, speaking in human terms, the New Testament knows only of a mother of Jesus. Jesus' ties with mankind are established through a woman only, through his mother, according to the New Testament evidence. If one dismisses the picture presented in the infancy narratives as untrue or as unhistorical or as a mere theologoumenon, the only alternative which is left, in terms of the New Testament evidence as well as of any (later) evidence, is that Jesus is a bastard and His mother a woman of ill repute.

This alternative impression would be heightened by the persistent reference to "the brothers of the Lord" who are often associated with Mary in the same texts, as well as by the fact that, except for Mt and Lk in the infancy narratives (cfr Jn), no reference is made to Mary's marital state. That the authors of the New Testament were of this shameful conviction, and that this was the message they wanted to convey to their readers, is extremely hard to believe. The mere fact that they did not bother to avoid this impression on their audience—of which they must have been aware—is an indication that in their minds there was no danger that the faithful would be led to draw such a debasing conclusion from their statements. This, in turn, could indicate that not only the writers of the New Testament but also their readers had some cognizance of Christ's origins. This also could explain why the name of Joseph or of any human father of Jesus plays no important role in the Christian tradition in general, and why it is altogether ignored even by Mk and Paul.

INFANCY NARRATIVES IN MT AND LK

The explicit testimony of Jesus' virginal conception by Mary is generally believed to be found in the infancy narratives of both Mt and Lk. Admittedly, even if the fact is granted, the immediate conclusion would be that Jesus' virginal conception was the conviction or faith of the evangelists and, perhaps, of the communities to whom they addressed themselves. From a theological point of view, the conviction of the evangelists expressed under the guidance of divine inspiration would be sufficient guarantee for a Christian faith to accept what God's word intends to teach man. Historically, however, various questions can be raised. The first is whether or not the narratives in Mt and Lk do really say that these evangelists were convinced of a virginal conception. It has always been accepted that this is in fact the conviction of Mt. Concerning Lk, however, some doubts have been expressed recently. It is here that the theologoumenon theory comes in.

Fitzmyer[100] notes that "four points may seem to militate against" the understanding of the annunciation scene in Luke in the sense of a virginal conception. 1) Mary's query in Lk 1:34 "How will this be, since I do not know man?" A query that Fitzmyer understands—correctly in my opinion—as "merely a Lucan stage-prop for the dramatization of the identification of the child," which, he says, should not be construed as a historicization. 2) The operation of the Holy Spirit in Lk 1:35: the "Holy Spirit will come upon you, and the power of the Most High will overshadow you." "The language used by the angel" —Fitzmyer says (569)—"is highly figurative, but neither verb . . . has in itself any connotation of conception, let alone of sexual implication" (?). The author maintains that the activity of the Spirit "does not exclude the idea of a miraculous conception." But it does "not say it either; least of all in an exclu-

100 'The Virginal Conception,' 567.

sive sense implying no human intervention." 3) The detail in Lk 2:5 "where we are told that Joseph went to Bethlehem to be enrolled in the census 'with Mary, his betrothed, who was with child.' " The pre-Lucan state of the sources "may suggest that this verse is not even to be thought of in terms of virginal conception. In any case, Luke 2:5 is hardly a strong argument in favor of Mary's virginity in the Lucan infancy narrative" (571). 4) The remark in Lk 3:23 where the evangelist notes that Jesus "was supposed" to be the son of Joseph. If "Luke suggests here Joseph's 'legal' or 'putative' paternity, what does that say about the divine filiation at the end? On the other hand, if one were to insist that it refers merely to the beginning of the genealogy, then there might be a significant corrective to it in the light of chap. 1" (572).

The conclusion is that in Luke the virginal conception "is a possibility that cannot be excluded. But in the long run, the Lucan Gospel does not assert the virginal conception of Jesus as clearly as does the Matthean annunciation scene" (572).

Whether Mt or Lk is more or less explicit in asserting the virginal conception of Jesus may be a matter of personal appreciation and evaluation. At any rate, in order not to prejudice the meaning of Lk's narrative it is this narrative that is considered in the first place; furthermore, it will be considered on its own merits, i.e. mainly within the framework of Lk's infancy narratives, and, occasionally, within the trends of the third Gospel.

From an historical viewpoint, the basis of all research for our discussion is the document itself as it is accessible to us. The document, for our purpose, is the narrative in Lk 1–2, which is accessible to us only in the form that the third evangelist integrated it into his Gospel.[101] An analysis of this document in its present form will disclose what the thought of the evangelist was at the time he wrote his Gospel. We may confidently say also, that such an analysis discloses not only the thought of the evangelist at that time, but also the belief of at least a certain segment of the Christian community, i.e., the church to which the evangelist belonged or wrote his Gospel, or both. For the recovery of the historical datum we have some sort of guarantee in a correct reading of the document as it is preserved in Lk.

Beyond that, the question can be raised as to whether the evangelist himself is the original author of the document or whether he adopted and adapted (to what extent?) a previous narrative. Another possible question is whether or not various sources (of possible different orientations) were integrated into the one narrative we possess either by Luke or by someone else before him. A reliable answer to these questions would disclose to us the situation about the belief in the virginal conception some time before the composition of the third Gospel. Legitimate as they may be, however, for obvious reasons these questions can be given conjectural and unreliable answers only. That is why the reading of the present document as it is today is given priority in our analysis.

The infancy narratives in Lk present a highly sophisticated structure, which also includes a chronological arrangement of

---

[101] An excellent monography about Lk 1–2 was written by Graystone Geoffrey, *Virgin of All Virgins. The Interpretation of Luke 1: 34,* (Rome 1968).

the material and a deliberate orientation to, and connection with, the beginning of the Gospel proper in Lk 3. The first narrative (1:5–25) deals with the annunciation about John the Baptizer who is promised to, and begotten by, a couple of old spouses beyond the age and the physical possibility (sterility, v. 7) of begetting children; this narrative leads up to the (end of the) fifth month of Elizabeth's pregnancy (v. 24).

The events of the second narrative (1:26–56) take place "in the sixth month" (v. 26) of Elizabeth's pregnancy. The evangelist insists on this chronological detail in v. 36. This second narrative deals with the annunciation about Jesus who is promised to a *parthenos,* virgin, who is involved in a marital situation with Joseph. Closely connected with the annunciation about Jesus is the visitation of Mary to Elizabeth, and Mary's song; in Luke's presentation this takes place before John's birth. In point of fact, this narrative carries the story further to the time of John's birth, since Mary remained with Elizabeth "about three months" (v. 56).

Accordingly, the third narrative (1:57–80) reports John's birth and some episodes related to it. In this section v. 80 is important because it certainly establishes a link between the infancy narratives and Lk 3:1–20, i.e., with the traditional beginning of the Gospel history. The fourth narrative (2:1–21) deals with the birth of Jesus and other episodes connected with it. V. 21 refers to the circumcision of the child on the "eighth day" from his birth.

After this, some other episodes follow which have no correspondence in John's history, but which are reported in some chronological sequence, and in preparation for the Gospel tradition in the rest of the book. The "days of purification" (2:22) were fulfilled on the fortieth day from birth (Lev 2:2–4). To Jesus' growth as a "child" reference is made in 2:40, and the episode in vv. 41–50 takes place when Jesus was "twelve years old" (v. 42). Then he continues to mature (v. 52)—probably until he "was about thirty" (3:23). In 2:39 and 2:51 the evangelist notes that Jesus went to live in Nazareth, which, no doubt, marks a connection with 4:16 where Nazareth is described as the place "where he was brought up" (not "born").

This cursory survey was made in order to show that there is in these narratives of Luke a unity of purpose and of design. If Luke used written sources he certainly made them serve a definite plan and direction. This unity of purpose is further evidenced by some sort of "cross references," besides the chronological sequence. Thus 1:36 is a reference to 1:24f; 1:41 refers to 1:15; the entire episode of the visitation (1:39–45) refers to the main themes in the foregoing narratives (Elizabeth's and Mary's maternity); 1:62–64 points back to 1:20–22; 1:76 is an interpretation of 1:15–17; 2:4–5 harks back to 1:26f; 2:19 is re-echoed in 2:51, and both passages have a correspondence in 1:66; 2:21 is a "quote" of 1:31; 239 ("went back" to Nazareth) refers to 2:4f and to 1:26f, and points to 2:51. More subtle theological contacts are spread throughout the entire chapters 1 and 2.

Mary, not a Wife

When Luke's material in these narratives is read with our particular problem in mind, the most obvious characteristic is the parallelism established by the evangelist (whoever he may be) between John's annunciation (1:5–25) and birth (1:57–80), on the one hand, and Jesus' annunciation and related episodes (1:26–56) and birth (2:1–21), on the other.[102] This symmetric disposition and tacit comparison of both series of events is generally admitted—it is obvious, in fact.

Now, the different way in which Elizabeth and Mary are introduced is certainly striking. According to the usual and normal practice, Elizabeth is presented as the "wife" (*gyne*)

---

102 See George Augustin, 'Le parallèle entre Jean-Baptiste et Jésus en Lc 1–2,' *Mélanges Bibliques en hommage au R. P. Béda Rigaux* (Gembloux. 1970) 147–171. The author thinks that the parallelism between John and Jesus is the work of Luke himself. Benoit Pierre, 'L'Enfance de Jean-Baptiste selon Lc I,' *NTS* 3 (1956/7) 169–194, would agree.

of Zachariah: Zachariah had a wife from among the daughters of Aaron (1:5); "your wife Elizabeth will bear a son *to
you*" (1:13); "my wife is advanced in age" (1:18); "his wife
Elizabeth conceived" (1:24). Significantly enough, Mary is not
introduced as the "wife" of Joseph or of anyone else, neither
when she is mentioned for the first time (1:27) nor when she
gives birth to Jesus (2:5) nor in the entire infancy narratives—
nor in the entire Gospel of Luke. On the contrary, the relationship of Mary to Joseph is expressed in a somewhat unusual way:
the very first time that Mary is mentioned she is introduced to
the readers as "a *parthenos* (virgin) betrothed/wedded (*emnesteumene*) to a man called Joseph"; Luke insists again that Mary
was a *parthenos* when he spells out her name (1:27). The very
first time Elizabeth is introduced to the reader, Luke characterizes her as "wife" of Zachariah, and this remains her characterization throughout the narrative. Both the description of Mary
as *parthenos* and, in connection with it, her relationship to
Joseph as a *emnesteumene* sounds strange, if Mary is in fact
Joseph's wife in the normal sense of the term. When this
presentation of Mary is compared with that of Elizabeth, one
gets the impression that Luke makes a deliberate effort in order
not to give his readers the impression that Mary was Joseph's
wife in the usual sense.

This impression is further confirmed by Lk 2:5. Even at the
time when she "was with child" and was about to give birth
to Jesus, Mary is called "*the* one betrothed/wedded" to Joseph:
this man went to Judah to be enrolled "with Mary *te emnesteumene auto.*" The evangelist's design is all the more obvious
here, because the most natural and spontaneous expression
would be "wife": he went with Mary his wife who was with
child. And yet, Luke refrains from saying so, and resorts to a
rather unusual, and certainly less natural replacement. Elizabeth
is never described in this way. That such is the evangelist's
concern can be seen in his accuracy to notice that, even though
Mary was with Joseph and was betrothed/wedded to him, she

gives birth to "her" son[103] (2:7)—in the entire narrative (in ch. 1–2) there is nothing like "their" son or Joseph's son. On the contrary, concerning Zachariah, "your wife will bear a *son to you*" (1:13).

The way Mary is introduced by Luke leads us deeper into our subject. The relationship between Mary and Joseph is expressed by the Greek term *mnesteuein,* which in the non-biblical Greek, when it applies to a man, means to seek (a woman) in marriage, to betroth (her), to marry (her); the woman is sought etc., and, in this case, the verb is used in the passive voice, as in our case. According to Lk 2:5 Mary is "the one betrothed/wedded" to Joseph. Fitzmyer[104] notes that this "description of Mary is dependent on 1:27." The dependence is obvious, to a considerable extent at least. But it is the presentation of Mary in 1:27, 28 that is most striking: Luke characterizes Mary as a *parthenon emnesteumenen andri,* as "a virgin betrothed/wedded to a man called Joseph." The important point is the association of a "virgin" with a betrothed/wedded situation—a situation that, as it is known, does not respond exactly to any of our marital provisions.

This description of Mary in Lk 1:27 is a technical expression of the Jewish marital law. The evidence for this comes from Deut 22:23 in the Greek translation, which in this case is a faithful rendering of the Hebrew text. Compare Lk and Deut.

Lk	Deut
parthenos emnesteumene[105] *andri*	*parthenos memnesteumene andri*

The realization that we have to deal with legal language is important for various reasons. First of all, this expression indicates a (particular) *marital status* of the persons involved. A woman in this situation is not defined just as a virgin (physical-

---

[103] The Greek is even stronger.
[104] 'The Virginal Conception,' 570.
[105] Many manuscripts have *memnesteumene,* which makes no difference.

ly), but she is defined as a "betrothed/wedded virgin," as a virgin involved in a marital situation: in fact, she is a virgin who is a "wife" (*'isshah,* LXX *gyne*: Deut 22:24). This emerges with all clarity from the context in Deut 22, where four marital situations of a woman are accurately distinguished: a) a woman who is "taken" (v. 13) to her husband's house (cfr v. 21) and they have relations for the first time (vv. 13–21); b) the married woman who is living with her husband (v. 22); c) the "girl virgin betrothed/wedded to a man" (v. 23), who also is called "a betrothed/wedded girl" (v. 25) or a "betrothed/wedded virgin" (v. 27)—all of them are legal terms; d) the "non-betrothed/wedded girl virgin" (v. 28)—what we call a "single" girl; Ex 25:15 calls this girl a *parthenon amnesteuton,* an unbetrothed virgin. Accordingly, Mary was a "betrothed/wedded virgin," she was in this particular relationship to Joseph; the purpose of the evangelist is not only to stress Mary's virginity (see below), but also to give information about her marital status: she was not a single virgin, she was a "wife-virgin."

What this marital status implied in the Jewish society is well known. The text in Deut 22:24 regards a betrothed virgin as a "wife." A Jewish commentator on Deut 22:20 notes that "betrothal . . . in ancient times carried with it almost all the legal consequences of marriage.[106] Strack and Billerbeck[107] confirm this statement: "In the Jewish view, through betrothal the union of a man and of a woman in marriage is juridically complete in every respect. Therefore the betrothed bride, *arusah,* is called the man's "wife," *issah,* she can become a widow, she is subjected to the Levirate law, she is dismissed through a document of divorce, as a widow or a divorcee she claims her *ketubbah,*[108] just as the married woman does; as the latter, she also

---

[106] *The Soncino Chumash,* ed. by Cohen A. (London, 1968) (seventh reprint), 1103.
[107] *Kommentar zum NT,* II, 374, 393f.
[108] Document of marriage contract.

is punished because of adultery . . . Some time after betrothal the bridegroom requests the bride to move over into his house for marriage (proper). From the time of this request a virgin was granted 12 months in the house of her parents . . . a widow was granted one month term."

Such is the situation of Mary according to the terms of the evangelist: she was a "betrothed/wedded virgin." And it is to this marital status that the Greek participle *emnesteumene* refers, at least when the angel addresses Mary in Lk 1:26–38, which was translated by "betrothed/wedded" because it implies both notions to a certain degree. This is the situation of the "bride-wife" (*nymphe-gyne*) to which Apc 21:9 (cfr v. 2) refers. The rabbinic language has a term to describe a woman in this marital situation: *arusah*. This is precisely the verbal root used in Deut 22:23, 25, 27 for "a virgin betrothed/wedded to a man," as well as in Deut 22:28; Ex 22:15 for a single "virgin not-betrothed/wedded"; and it is to this root and concept that *mnesteuesthai* corresponds both in Lk 1:27 (at least) and, most of the time, in the LXX. In this perspective, it is even more striking that Luke refrains from calling Mary Joseph's wife, which he could legitimately do, even in 1:27, according to the Jewish legal language. But, then it is all the more significant that he does not call Mary "wife" in 2:5, where he insists on calling her "the" *arusah* (bride-wife) of Joseph.

The realization that Mary's presentation as "a virgin *arusah* of Joseph" is legal marital language, is important in our discussion for another reason. The Greek term *parthenos* (virgin) cannot be understood here as "girl." The evidence for this comes precisely from Deut 22:23, 25, 27, 28, from where Lk's language comes. Where Lk uses *parthenos*—which also is the translation of the LXX—the Hebrew text uses the specific term *betulah*, which leaves no doubt as to the specific quality of virginity.[109] It is all the more so that in all these passages of Deut

[109] The legal character of the formula is an additional reason why *parthenos*, virgin, in Lk 1, 27 cannot be considered a later insertion.

the concept of "girl" is present also, but it is expressed by another term, *naarah* (LXX, *pais, neanis*), which, according to Strack and Billerbeck,[110] indicates the "normal time for the betrothal" of a woman, "i.e. of a virgin between 12 and 12 and a half years"; it also becomes a legal term. Besides this, the text in Deut 22 makes a distinction between a "woman espoused to a spouse" (husband) (*beulat baal;* LXX, *synokismene andri*) (v. 22), a "girl virgin" who is an *arusah* (v. 23), and a "girl virgin" who is not an *arusah* (v. 28). Obviously, in the first case the term *betulah* is missing; in the third case, which is confirmed by Ex 22:15, the notion *betulah* certainly stresses the concept of an unbetrothed virgin; now, the same term, and in the same context, is used of the girl who is neither "married" (espoused to a spouse) nor unbetrothed—but is an *arusah*. And the context in vv. 13–21 makes it abundantly clear that in an *arusah* the "tokens of virginity" are to be found.

All this is evidence that when Mary is introduced as a "virgin *arusah*" of Joseph in Lk 1:27, she is thought of, not in terms of a girl, but in terms of a *betulah,* The result is that the "tokens of virginity" were to be found in her, the quality of her physical virginity is explicitly brought into relief by the very terms used by the evangelist. And this also applies when "the name of the *parthenos,* virgin, was Mary." In this case *parthenos* is the shorthand for the entire expression "virgin *arusah*," so that it cannot be translated by girl.

That Lk understands *parthenos* in very strict terms, receives some further support from the way he introduces Anne in 2:36f —an introduction which in many respects is reminiscent of that of Elizabeth: Anne, who is old and a widow at eighty-four years, "had been living with a husband (cfr Deut 22:22) from her *parthenias,*" which is understood as "from the time she was a virgin" by Ardnt-Gingrich;[111] in fact, the same authors understand that this Greek word means "virginity as a

---

[110] Strack H.-Billerbeck P., *Kommentar zum NT,* II, 374f.
[111] Under *apo* II 1 a.

state."[112] That the word expresses strict virginity can be seen in 4 Macc 4:7f and in Sir 42:10.

That the physical virginity of Mary is the purpose of the narrative, derives not only from the terms themselves, but also from the very marital status of Mary. It is obvious, in fact, that the legal phrase used by the evangelist presents Mary in the state of the Jewish betrothal (*erusin* or *qiddushin*). Though betrothed to a husband (cfr Lk 2:36), she was not an *isshah beulat baal* (a wife espoused to a spouse), she had yet to show the tokens of virginity. This, in its turn, implies that she was still living with her relatives, not with her husband. The fact, furthermore, that she, otherwise than Elizabeth (1:7, 18, 36; cfr 1:25), is not said to have proved being unfruitful or to be old—or widow—indicates that she was a *naarah betulah,* a young virgin. A betrothed virgin was normally granted twelve months before being taken into her husband's house. This seems to be the perspective adopted in the narrative of Lk 1:26–40: during the annunciation Joseph seems to be absent, at least he plays no role; Mary is free to travel to Zachariah's house, apparently without Joseph; she can remain there as long as "some three months" (1:40)—whereafter she "goes back to *her* house" (see the difference in 2:39, 51). For all this time she had not been taken into Joseph's house.

Mother: But How?

Such is the setting in which Lk stages the narrative of the annunciation: right at the beginning he points out that there was "a virgin betrothed to a man called Joseph, and the virgin's name was Mary." This sets the pattern to read and understand what follows in the narrative of the annunciation and, we may safely say, in the rest of the infancy narratives.

Of course, one of the points which stand out in the present discussion is Mary's query in v. 34: "How *will* this *be,* since I do not know (any) man." No doubt, this has to be understood

[112] Under *parthenia.*

within the setting described at the beginning. It can be agreed that Mary's query is designed to give the angel an opening for further defining the meaning of his message and the character of the child.[113] But this "dialectic" role does not empty Mary's expression of a "logical" content—its dialectic role exists in as much as its logical content is maintained. It is still important, therefore, to learn the meaning of Mary's query; there can be no doubt that through it the evangelist intended to express some thought.[114] Refraining from doing so amounts to going around the problem.

Fitzmyer notes that Mary's question was explained in different ways down through the centuries: apart from what he calls "some contorted explanations," he mentions the understanding of the question in the sense of a vow, resolve or intention of refraining from marital intercourse, and the understanding in the sense of a protest because she had not yet had such an experience. Then Fitzmyer refers to the understanding as a "surprise because she is not yet married (which implies—Fitzmyer goes on to say—that Mary understood the angel's words to mean a conception that was already under way, as in parallel angelic communications in the OT, and one which the further words of the angel clarify and refer to the future) . . . the least forced explanation seems to be the third, surprise at the announcement that is understood in the OT sense that conception is already under way."[115]

Actually this third interpretation of a conception already under way is precisely the one about which we can be sure that it is discarded by the evangelist himself. The message of the angel also includes the name of the child: Jesus (1:31). Now,

---

[113] Even though this purely 'dialectic' role of the expression is not without difficulties: cfr Graystone G., *Virgin of all Virgins,* 104f.

[114] Lattke Gisela, 'Lukas 1 und die Jungfrauengeburt,' *Jungfrauengeburt* (Stuttgart, 1970) 82: "The understanding of the question must be determined according to the answer: the author puts it on Mary's lips so that the meaning of what is promised in v. 35 is clear to everyone."

[115] Fitzmyer J., 'The Virginal Conception,' 567f.

according to Lk 2:21, when the child was circumcised, he was called Jesus; the name "which was expressed by the angel *before he* (the child) *was conceived in the womb.*" The reference to the angel's message in Lk 1:31 is unmistakable. Therefore, this message, which is a part of the annunciation narrative, took place "before the child was conceived."[116] But there is more. In Mary's question the evangelist uses the future tense: "How will this be?" (*estai*), which, to use a less formal expression, means this: "how is this going to be." In Lk's mind Mary's question is not an expression of surprise or of protest—but of real "business": Mary's inquiry refers to the specific way in which her maternity is going to take place. Furthermore, in the entire section, vv. 31–35, the message of the angel is phrased in the future tense: just as Mary "will give birth, will name the child," just as the child "will be great, will be called (vv. 31, 35), will rule," and just as the Lord "will give him the throne"—so also Mary "*will* conceive"[117] and also the Spirit "*will* come upon Mary, and *will* overshadow her." The entire narrative is projected into the future, conception itself not excluded.[118]

Why the Power of the Most High?

To this future perspective the activity of the Spirit belongs. The reference to the Spirit is in answer to Mary's question "how

---

[116] A reason already pointed out by the old 'catenae'; cfr Bauer J. B., 'Philologische Bemerkungen zu Lk 1, 34,5 *Bib* 45 (1964) 539.

[117] As for the efforts to understand this future tense in a present or even past sense, cfr Graystone G., *Virgin of All Virgins*, 89–93.

[118] Mary's question, therefore, has to be related to the entire narrative which is conceived in a 'future' perspective, and not just to the notion 'to conceive' in 1, 31 that Bauer J. B., 'Philologische Bemerkungen,' 535–540, maintains was an ambivalent Hebrew participle which was mistakenly translated by a future. Against this understanding, which is the basis of the 'surprise' explanation, serious objections have been raised by Gewiss Joseph, 'Die Marienfrage, Lk 1, 34,' *BZ* 5 (1961) 229–236. Cfr, furthermore, Lattke Gisela, 'Lukas 1 und die Jungfrauengeburt,' *Zum Thema Jungfrauengeburt* (Stuttgart, 1970) 65: against a present understanding of the verb "speak the verbs in v. 35 which obviously are in the future tense, as well as the Old Testament promises in the Septuagint concerning future conceptions . . ." (Judges 13, 5; Is 7, 14). Cfr fnt 117.

will this be" and is an alternative to a "knowledge of man"; in fact the angel "answers" (*apokrinesthai* has here its proper meaning) and speaks "to her" (v. 35). Of course, the action of the Spirit is not easy to define. Still, several elements are clear. It is only too obvious that it has no proper "sexual connotation" (which is not a discovery). The intervention of the Spirit will take place some time in the future; not at the present moment, not in the past. It is certainly related to the entire message of the narrative, i.e. to Mary's maternity. More specifically, it is an "answer" to Mary's question about the "how" of her maternity[119] as this "how" implies some sort of alternative to a "knowledge of man" (see below). The activity of the Spirit affects Mary directly and immediately; the implications for the child are an *additional* and derivative (*dio kai*) result of the answer to Mary's question; the first part of the angel's explanation in v. 35 answers directly and immediately such a question (*epi se, soi*). The activity of the Spirit does have a "connotation of conception"; in fact, from this activity (*dio*) something is "going to be begotten" which is a "son" (God's son); furthermore, the entire context shows that this is "how" Mary *"will conceive* in the womb and *bear a son"* (v. 31), her son. That much is clear.

The specific activity of the Spirit is expressed in these words: The "Holy Spirit will come upon (*eperchesthai*) you, and the power of the Most High will overshadow (*episkiazein*) you." Admittedly, the two verbs in this sentence "are otherwise unattested in a context that would suggest"[120] conception or sexual implication—this is true in Greek, see below. And this is

---

[119] Bauer J. B., ' "Pos" in ther Griechischen Bibel,' *NT* 2 (1957) 81–91, notes that rather than a question about 'how' the Greek *pos* opens a rhetoric question which in fact denies a given possibility. For Lk 1, 34 his translation is: "The intimated ('befohlen') conception is not possible, since I am not (yet) married" (p. 84). One wonders whether, in the last end, changing the question into a statement makes much difference. Furthermore, the reference to no knowledge of man certainly points in the direction of 'how'—and so does the explanation of the angel in v. 35 as well as the mention of God's power in v. 37.

[120] Fitzmyer J., 'The Virginal Conception,' 569.

an additional reason that the evangelist is suggesting a very unusual operation, since the connotation of conception is only too obvious in the present context; and unusual conceptions do not happen every day.

This unusual operation certainly requires "the power (*dynamis*) of the Most High." This is further stressed by the statement that "nothing shall be (fut.) impossible (*adynatein*) with God" (v. 36), which refers to the case of Mary, rather than to that of Elizabeth who "had conceived six months" earlier already. Moreover, after having realized her maternity (1:42f), Mary understands that it was "the Powerful" one (*ho dynatos*) who did "great things to her" (1:49). This "power," it should be recalled, is connected with Mary's conception and with a son who is "being begotten." Now, since Mary was a virgin in a strict sense, there is no evidence that she, unlike Elizabeth, was unfruitful; the evangelist, on the other hand, does not say that she or Joseph were old (which he says concerning Zachariah and Elizabeth); he rather implies that they were young, given their marital status where Mary is a virgin *arusah*. On the other hand, there were no doubts about Mary being able to find a husband, since she was already betrothed/wedded, and normal marital life in the near future was open to her. In such a situation why should all that "power" be needed for Mary to conceive a child some time from now? Why should "the power of the Most High" and the intervention of "the Powerful" one be required for a child to be conceived and born of a young lady bound to join her husband at any time? It would have been a waste of power really, if Mary's conception were not an extraordinary, wonderful conception; that is, in fact, what the "great things the Powerful did to her," and to her only, mean in biblical language. Furthermore, if Mary's conception were not miraculous in some way, it would be a perfect anticlimax in reference to Elizabeth's pregnancy mentioned in this connection. If Mary is going to conceive of her husband, what is the use of referring to the (already visible) conception of an old and unfruitful woman? In point of fact, this reference is intended as a confirmation of "how" Mary's conception "is going to be": God has followed wondrous ways with Elizabeth, he can follow wondrous ways with Mary too. The ways are different, however. Concerning Elizabeth, God has multiplied his "compassion" (*eleos*) (1: 58) since he "took away her shame" (1.25). With Mary it is the "Powerful" God who is at work.

It is certainly within this framework that the notion of the Spirit-Power "coming upon" Mary and "overshadowing" her is to be understood. These verbs intend to suggest a "begetting" activity of God by which Mary conceives. Admittedly the notions are general in character, and it is the context which defines them, rather than conversely. But I would welcome a clear explanation about God's begetting power by anyone who understands, better than Luke understood and explained, how God works in case He decides to fertilize a woman Himself without man's intervention (nothing is impossible with God).[121]

But is it absolutely true that the notions used by Luke in this connection have no conceptional or sexual connotation in some way? A Jewish scholar[122] whose mastery of the biblical and Jewish literary expression is beyond question understands that the language used by Luke was inspired by Ruth 2:12: "I am Ruth your handmaid; spread therefore *your wing over* your handmaid for you are a redeemer," through the semantic connotations of the Aramaic words in the Jewish commentators. Concerning *episkiazein* in Luke 1:35,

---

[121] The linguistic choice of Luke, furthermore, has some theological overtones which agree very well with the present situation. The Spirit appears as a fertilizing power in Is 32, 15 so as to render a desolate land fruitful; again, Is 44, 3 in an obvious metaphor considers the Spirit as a fertilizing water which multiplies 'human' seed; cfr Is 51, 1–3; 41, 8. Benoit P., 'L'Annonciation,' *Exégèse et Théologie*, III (Paris, 1968) 206f, prefers the image suggested by Ps 91, 4; 104, 8 related to Ex 25, 20 etc., to conclude that the picture is that of a bird covering its eggs to bring forth life.

[122] Daube David, *The New Testament and Rabbinic Judaism* (London, 1956) 27–36.

it is an exact equivalent of Hebrew *salal* or Aramaic *tallel,* which, while literally denoting "to overshadow," is very often applied to the descent on a person or object of the divine presence . . . (p. 27) . . . the cloak worn by pious or scholarly men, and distinguished by "wings," borders, . . . called *tallith,* from the root *telal,* "shadow." Now the expression "to spread the *tallith* over a woman" is used in Rabbinic literature as a refined alternative for "to cohabit with a woman." We may safely assume that it was coined under the influence of two Old Testament passages: one Ezechiel, where God reminds Jerusalem how "Thy time was the time of love, and I spread my wings over thee," and the other Ruth's request "Spread thy wing." It follows that some Rabbis must have paraphrased this request by "Spread thy *tallith"*—which comes very near to "Overshadow" (p. 34).

Another point seems even more important. In the verses where Boaz addresses Ruth as having come "under the wings of God," the Aramaic version translates "under the *telal*—cover, shadow—of the Shekinah of his glory." Even the Hebrew comments of the Rabbis paraphrase "under the shadow—*sel*—of God". . . .

No doubt there were Aramaic versions translating "Spread thy wing" by "Spread the shadow of thy wing" or simply "Overshadow . . ." But even if there were no such versions, the rendering "Spread the shadow of thy wing" or "Overshadow" was the appropriate one as soon as the scene was transferred to a higher sphere, of the kind to be found in Luke. Quite possibly, the mention of "the power" of God, the *dynamis,* is also connected with this elevation to a higher sphere. The Rabbis, where they wish to avoid bluntness, resort to euphemisms like "to lay one's power (*reshut*) over a woman" . . . (p. 34).

It only remains to add that Mary's words, "Behold the handmaid of the Lord," are still from the same source. "I am Ruth thine handmaid . . ." (p. 36).

The author notes, furthermore, that at that moment, Ruth was not yet married to Boaz; her request really means "May you take me to wife," which, far from being immodest was understood by the Rabbis as agreeing "with the most refined notions of morality" (p. 33). On the other hand, "In Rabbinic literature . . . Boaz sometimes stands for God himself, or at least speaks and acts as God himself would" (p. 33). The text from Ruth contains also the expression "for you are a redeemer": "It is obvious that here was a most suitable expression for the New Testament narrative" (p. 34). On this view Ford has elaborated very recently.[123]

No Knowledge of Man

Within the evangelist's understanding about "how will this be," the rest of Mary's question is to be explained: "since I do not know man" or a husband (*epei andra ou ginosko*).[124] First of all, this expression provides the reason why the first part of the question is asked: how is this going to be "since (seeing that)[125] I do not know man?" Secondly, the pronoun "this" refers to the entire process disclosed in the annunciation —conception and childbirth included; even more, conception and childbirth are particularly intended, as it is evidenced by the "non-knowledge of man," i.e. this knowledge refers to "marital" relations. Thirdly, the non-knowledge of man is related to something which is going to take place some time in the *future* (*estai*), in accordance with the perspective in the entire narrative ("before the child was conceived": 2:21). The question is this: how is she going to conceive a child "since I

---

[123] Ford Massingberd J., 'Mary's Virginitas Post-Partum and Jewish Law,' *Bib* 54 (1973) 269–272:" . . . the narrative of the Annunciation is presented in terms of a betrothal or marriage contract or marital consummation, the proposal made by God and the acceptance expressed by Mary. The event had been foreshadowed in the book of Ruth . . . through her voluntary consent Mary had become the property of God for all time. She would be 'forbidden to the whole world' for God had chosen her like a consecrated vessel—or the ark—in the sanctuary. In this way no disparagement is cast upon physical marital union: for the Jews this was a sacred act. However, God invited Mary to a new way of life, one of total commitment such as has not been envisaged previously in Judaism. One could say that Is 54, 5 was fully realized."

[124] But not "my" husband cfr Graystone G. *Virgin of all Virgins*, 118ff.

[125] Liddle-Scott, *epei* B.

do not know any man." Fourthly, the non-knowledge of man, as it is stated, certainly emphasizes the present condition of Mary as virgin physically, which agrees with her marital status and with her presentation as a virgin by the evangelist; this is certainly the main concern of the evangelist who intends to teach something about Jesus rather than about Mary. Fifthly, the difference between Mary's question and Zachariah's—both formulated by the same evangelist—is relevant: the latter asks "by what is he going to know" that the promise of the angel is reliable; he asks for a sort of guarantee that he can rely on a promise which seems unattainable to him, given the existing circumstances. Mary asks about the "how,"[126] about the way in which the message *will* become true; obviously, she does not see any problem about the "what," about her conceiving a son. In fact, the reasons why these questions are asked are different also. Zachariah asks for some sort of token *because* both he and his wife are old (besides Elizabeth's unfruitfulness, 1:7), the suggestion being that the conditions of nature do not add to the credibility of the promise. Mary merely asks about the "how" of her motherhood *since* she does not know man, the suggestion being that, in her case, the conditions of nature itself are open to the "what," and the factual possibility is precluded only by Mary's attitude—whatever it may be—towards man (husband). Sixthly, in the perspective of the evangelist, the conception itself—even though subsequent to the annunciation, 2:21—takes place shortly after Mary's acceptance (1:38), since "some three months" before the birth of John (who was in his sixth month of gestation by the time of Mary's annunciation, 1:36), Mary is declared mother by the evangelist through Elizabeth (1:42f), and the evidence of her maternity is the gift of the Spirit which is given through her (1:41 in reference to 1:15); after this, in fact, the references to Mary's maternity are in past tenses—God "has looked upon his servant" and "has

126 About the meaning of this "how," cfr Graystone G., *op.c.,* 107–112.

done great things to her" (1:48)—which are projected against the future tenses of the annunciation. Now, in the process of conception Joseph is conspicuously ignored. In the case of John "Zachariah went home; and after these days Elizabeth *his wife* conceived" (1:23f). Nothing similar is said of Mary's conception. As pointed out above, the perspective of the evangelist is rather that, for all this time, Mary still lived alone, she first appears in Joseph's company on her journey to Bethlehem (2:4).

The meaning of Mary's question, therefore, is bound by the elements of this setting which would seem undeniable in the design of the evangelist. Admittedly, Mary's statement is formulated in a *present* tense: *ou ginosko,* "I do not know" (man). Still this present is the reason of a future event ("how will this be"), which includes conception itself (cfr 2:21). If the "non-knowledge of man"[127] were to be restricted to the present moment, a question about the "how" of conception, and the reason for this question (I do not know man) would be meaningless both logically and literarily. Given her marital situation, Mary was to join her husband in the near future. To pretend that a present "non-knowledge of man" would be an obstacle for a (natural) "how" in the future is to make Mary, or rather the evangelist, too childish and illogical. Obviously, according to the evangelist the "how" of what is going to happen in the future is conditioned to the fact that Mary "does not know man."

Mary's expression is an obvious Hebrew idiom. It is well known that in the biblical language a paraphrase to describe a virgin *stricto sensu* is this: "a woman who did not know man"[128] (Gen 19:8; Jud 11:39, see v. 37; 21:12; basically the same are Num 31:18, 35; Jud 21:11; cfr. Wisd 3:13)—which,

[127] Nothing changes if "man" is to be translated as (betrothed) husband: Bauer J. B., 'Philologische Bemerkungen,' 535 (but cfr fnt 124).

[128] Which, as Graystone G., *op.c.,* 118, rightly remarks, "indicates not simply that a person is unmarried, whether betrothed or not, but that she has experienced no sexual relations, is *virgo intacta.*"

incidentally, shows that the same expression in Lk 1:34 points to virginity proper. These are all passages where the Bible refers to women who "did not know man." Interestingly enough, however, the present tense is never used in such a connection even though the actual condition of virginity in those women is intended in all these passages (except perhaps Wisd 3:13). The Hebrew text invariably uses the perfect tense (Jud 11:39), even in the cases of direct speech like Gen 19:8; Num 31:18; and the Greek translation invariably uses the aorist tense. Against this background the present tense in Lk 1:34 is certainly striking.[129]

But in the Old Testament we also find the active participle *yodaat* to express the lasting condition of a woman who has had relations with some man; this is a woman "who knows man"; in this case not the perfect tense but the active participle *yodaat* is used in the two cases where this description is found: Num 31:17 (note the contrast in v. 18) and Jud 21:11. Of course, it is not the condition indicated by this formula that is of any interest to us, but rather the linguistic expression which indicates this lasting condition as open-ended. In these two passages the Hebrew participle is translated into Greek by the perfect in Num 31:17, and by a present participle (*ginoskousa*) in Jud 21:11. But the same Hebrew participle is also translated by the present of *ginoskein* (Gen 33:13; Ps 1:6; 36:11; 37:18; 44:22; Koh 11:6 etc.) or of *eidenai* (Ruth 3:11; 1 Sam 23:17; 2 Chron 2:7; Esth 4:14, etc.) very often.

---

[129] The contention of Quecke Hans, 'Lk 1, 34 in den alten Übersetzungen und im Protevangelium des Jakobus,' *Bib* 44 (1963) 500ff, that the present tense in Lk can be translated as a past tense, breaks down when contrasted with this philological and linguistic fact. He contends (p. 503), furthermore, that in Judges 21, 11.12 the Hebrew expression either in perfect or in participle "can express the same fact" or situation. This does not seem to be true. Judges 21, 11 (part.) expresses a lasting present or situation which derives from experiences (intercourse) in the past; the (Hebr.) perfect in v. 12 (aor. in Greek) connotes one first act in the past: a woman who *never* knew man, never had such an experience yet. Quecke's note, 'Lk 1, 34 im Diatessaron,' *Bib* 65 (1964) 85–88 does not change anything. Cfr the difficulties raised by Bauer J. B., 'Philologische Bemerkungen,' 535–540.

The formula of Lk 1:34, therefore, is the same formula of Num 31:17 and of Jud 21:11 with the only difference of a negative connotation. When one realizes that the Greek *epei* (Lk 1:34) often translates the Hebrew *kî* (Ex 1:21; Josh 17: 13; Jud 6:7; 1 Sam 1:5; Job 7:12, etc.), the semitic re-translation of Mary's expression is easy: *kî enenni yodaat îsh,* in Hebrew—and a virtually identical sentence in Aramaic—where the active participle of the Hebrew root is used.[130] Now, it is well known that both in Hebrew and in Aramaic the active participle is like an adjective and indicates the action it expresses "as a state, i.e., in its lasting aspect," and it stresses not only the present time but also, very often, the near future or even future in general.[131] It is this understanding which not

---

[130] The participle *yodaat* is precisely the translation of this passage used by Delitsch Franz in his Hebrew translation of the New Testament; Cfr Graystone G., *op.c.,* 124.

[131] Joüon Paul, *Grammaire de l'hébreu biblique* (2d ed., Rome, 1947) a. c.: "In Hebrew . . . the participle is an atemporal form, i.e. it can be indistinctively used in the three temporal spheres: present, future, past . . . used as predicate (this is our case) the participle has something of an adjective nature. From the viewpoint of time, above all and as by its own nature the participle expresses the present. It is by an extension of its use as present that the participle is very often used for the near future or even for the future in general." Similar terms in Brockelmann Carl, *Hebräische Syntax* (Neukirchen, 1956) 45f. As for the Aramaic, cfr Levy Jacob, *Chaldäisches Wörterbuch über die Targumin* (Leipzig, 1881): *'id* . . . agrees completely in all its meanings with the Hebrew.' Bauer H.-Leander P., *Grammatik des Biblisch-Aramäisch* (Halle, 1927) 290f: "When it is treated as a noun, the participle does not have any reference to a definite time; but when its verbal character is intended, as a rule the active participle by its own nature indicates the sphere of the present, the passive participle that of the perfect" . . . The active participle is used "in the function of the future . . . (in fnt 2) cfr the Jewish Palestinian Aramaic, where this (future) use is predominant, particularly so in the language of the Palestinian Talmud, and has almost excluded the aorist from this role." Cfr Rowley H. H., *The Aramaic of the Old Testament* (Oxford, 1929) 98; Schlesinger Michael, *Satzlehre der Aramäischen Sprache des Babylonischen Talmuds* (Leipzig, 1928) 40.—The view is often expressed that v 34 is an addition by Luke to a preexisting narrative (cfr recently Schneider Gerhard, 'Jesu geistgewirkte Empfängnis (Lk 1, 34f). Zur Interpretation einer christologischen Aussage,' *Theologisch-Praktische Quartalschrift* 119 (1971) 107f. The perfectly semitic idiom, however, does not support such a view.

only fits into the context but is demanded by this context on account of the future perspective of the narrative in general and of the very marital situation of Mary who was supposed to join her husband in the near future. The philological understanding of Mary's objection indicates that "she is not going to know man."[132] I am not concerned with the question here whether the expression implies a vow, promise or determination of a virginal life nor whether a marriage in such an understanding is a true marriage. What is sure, however, is that the evangelist wrote such an expression to stress that Mary was a virgin at the time of the annunciation and that she was going to be a virgin for the near future, i.e. at the time when she was to conceive Jesus: she was not going to know man.[133] The evangelist wanted to express something with this sentence, and this is what the sentence means.[134]

Jesus and Isaac

Sometimes the passage in Gal 4:29 is mentioned in this connection to the effect that Mary's conception by the power of the Spirit does not necessarily imply a virginal conception. Gal 4:29, in fact says that Isaac was begotten or born *kata pneuma,* "according to the Spirit." But it is likely that "according to the Spirit" corresponds to "through the promise" in v. 23: Isaac was born not by the usually existing genetic capabilities

---

The semitic idiom is all the more to be noticed, since this is the only time that it occurs in Luke's writings (cfr Acts 21, 9: *parthenoi*)—and in the entire New Testament (1 Cor 7, 1 *haptesthai*).

[132] Mary's statement has been rightly illustrated with sentences such as "I do not smoke, I do not drink," which indicate both a present situation and an intention for the future.

[133] The purpose of him who wrote this sentence was not so much to stress Mary's intention or plans concerning her virginity in the future, as to teach that Christ was to be conceived virginally in the near future. In this perspective, the questions about a vow or about the validity of a marriage with a vow or determination of virginity do not arise.

[134] Cfr Latke G., 'Lukas 1' 82; Benoit Pierre, 'L'Annonciation,' 205. That Mary never was strongly attracted by marital life (cfr Zerwick M., '. . . quoniam virum non cognosco,' *VD* 37 (1959) 281 cannot be extracted from the sentence.

(*kata sarka*)—as they were summarized v.g. in Jn 1:13 (cfr. 3:6)—which are assumed not to exist in this case, but by a particular determination of God expressed in a promise, in the communication of which the Spirit is active (cfr 1 Cor 12:8, etc., Mt 22:43; Acts 4:25; 11:28; 2 Peter 1:21) so as to render the promise "inspired" and, thereby, guaranteed. The strict paralleism in v. 23 ("according to the flesh—through a promise") and v. 29 ("according to the flesh—according to the Spirit") in Gal 4 speaks for this understanding.[135]

It is more likely, however, that the clause "according to the Spirit" stresses the concept of God's power as, v.g., in Rom 1:4; and then Isaac is born, not by normal, genetic capabilities, but by God's power. But Paul's understanding is that this power was needed because Abraham realized that his body was as good as dead, for he was nearly a hundred years old, and that Sarah's womb was also dead; and hoping against hope, Abraham believed in the God who restores the dead to life, in the conviction that he who had promised is also powerful to accomplish (Rom 4:17–21). Not only Sarah's womb but also Abraham's body is involved; in fact, Paul points out very clearly that both the child born "according to the flesh" and the one born "according to the Spirit" are Abraham's children: "Abraham had two children, one by the servant woman and one by the freeborn wife" (Gal 4:22f). In the case of Jesus, there is no mention or suggestion that Mary (or Joseph) was hoping against hope or that either her womb or Joseph's body, or both, were dead. The opposite is the obvious assumption of the narrative, as well as of Mary's question: it is taken for granted that she was as able as Hagar to conceive "according to the flesh" whenever she decided to "know a man." Furthermore, in Lk's narrative Joseph's "body" or age is not taken into any consideration nor is it said that Joseph "had a child"—not even

---

[135] Cfr Nellessen E., *Das Kind* 107: "According to the Spirit" means, in Paul's language, "that Isaac is the son of the promise, that he 'lives of God's gracious assurance.'"

in Lk 2:7 where the evangelist deliberately points out that Mary
gave birth to "her" son (not to "their" or "his" son). Furthermore, the expression (to bear or beget) "according to the
Spirit" is not the same thing as the "overshadowing" of the
Spirit or the "coming upon" of the Power of the Most High—
nor is it the same thing as (being with child) "by (*ek*) the
Holy Spirit" (cfr Rom 1:3 *ek spermatos*) in Mt 1:18, 20.

It is obvious that the power of the Spirit can be needed and
can be effective in different cases and in different ways. The
particular context will tell the reason why this power is needed
and what is its effectiveness in each case. In Isaac's birth it was
the failure or limitation of nature which had to be "revived." In
Jesus' birth it was the very power and capability of nature which
was set in motion not by the normal process (which was available) but by a process which requires God's intervention precisely because the normal one is deliberately excluded even
though it is available.

Joseph with Mary, "the one betrothed to him"

In Lk 2:5 the evangelist records that Joseph went to Bethlehem in order to be registered together "with Mary *te emnesteumene auto,* the one betrothed to him." Fitzmyer[136] finds several
problems in this sentence. Of course, the main question is
whether the Greek expression transliterated should be understood as "fiancée" or as "wife." He agrees that some alternative
readings in the textual tradition are too weak and, as such,
negligible; the result being that we have to keep the reading
transliterated here. Fitzmyer's contention is that this expression
should be understood as "fiancée," or "engaged," not as wife—
and this is an important realization. But then he sees another
problem: "what is Mary doing in the company of Joseph on
a journey if she is still only "engaged"?[137] On the other hand,

---

[136] 'The Virginal Conception,' 570f.
[137] *Ibid.*

this author maintains that this "description of Mary (in 2:5) is dependent on 1:27 . . . it might seem to be a formulation made in the light of the virginal conception, but—he adds—it is not *per se* clear, and nothing else in ch. 2 favors it. No hint is given about the cause of Mary's pregnancy, and the original independence of Ch. 2 from Ch. 1 may suggest that this verse is not even to be thought of in terms of virginal conception."[138]

In the first place, Fitzmyer admits that the description of Mary as "the one betrothed to him," to Joseph, depends on 1:27. And this is precisely a proof that, at least at the level of Luke's composition, there is no independence of Ch. 2 from Ch. 1: the evangelist wrote 2:5 having 1:27 in mind. This remains true, whatever the basis for the original independence of these chapters—which, incidentally, is conjectural at best, and, as such, cannot provide solid ground for drawing any serious conclusion. In the second place, this reference to 1:27 explains why the cause of Mary's pregnancy is not given in 2:5. To every reader of the gospel the cause of Mary's pregnancy was clear after the narrative of the annunciation. No reason can be provided why Luke, or any other writer, should repeat the same concept several times.

It is precisely this reference to 1:27 and to the entire episode of the annunciation that accounts for the particular description of Mary as "the one betrothed to Joseph"—and not as his wife. The fact that Mary is in the company of Joseph on the way to Bethlehem is clear evidence that, according to the Jewish law and usage, at this moment Mary is no longer in the marital situation prevailing in 1:27–56. At this point (2:5) she was living with Joseph, juridically she was an *isshah beulat-baal* (Deut 22:22; cfr LXX), i.e., "a woman espoused to a spouse" (husband), with the meaning of "a woman married to a man." This is in perfect agreement both with the situation described in 1:27 and with the Jewish marital legislation and custom.

[138] *Ibid.*

Still, he who wrote Lk 2:5 has deliberately avoided calling Mary Joseph's wife.

This intention is all the more conspicuous when one realizes that a "betrothed" woman could be called "wife" even before she joined her husband. Evidence for this is Deut 22:24; Mt 1:20, 24 (v. 16 "husband") and the quotations found in Strack-Billerbeck.[139]

Furthermore, in the same context, Lk 2:6, Mary who was in Joseph's company, gives birth to "her" first born son—the son is "hers" and hers only; at the end of the episode, v. 7, Joseph is associated with Mary in one pronoun: there was no place for "them," still the child is "hers" only. The obvious expression of the biblical language in the case of a child born in normal wedlock would be that Mary bore a son *to Joseph:* "Elizabeth will bear *you* a son," Gabriel says to Zachariah (Lk 1:13; cfr. Gen 22:21). On the other hand, the evangelist stresses that Mary gave birth to "her first-born son," when Joseph is explicitly mentioned in the immediate context. This is certainly not biblical language. In the bible an individual is the first-born of his/her *father;* the bible *never* refers to someone as the first-born of his/her mother.[140] Were Mary's child the son of Joseph, the expression "Joseph's first-born" would be customarily (and perhaps even legally) imperative, if for some reason this quality had to be brought into relief. At any rate, in the case of John

---

[139] *Kommentar zum NT,* II, 393ff.

[140] Deut 21, 15.16.17 is no exception to this rule: it does not refer to the first-born son of his mother but to the father's first-born child who happens to be the son of the non-beloved wife. In 1 Chron 8, 30 the LXX offers an incorrect translation (Hebrew "his," not "her," first-born). In Ex 12, 29 the reference is to the first-born of the captive (man or woman); but the parallel passage Ex 11, 5 refers to the first-born of the maid-servant. The latter is the only case where reference is made to the first-born of a woman. But it is an exceptional case: probably the reference is to a "captive" maid—or concubine—where either paternity is unknown or irregular, or where the right of the first-born child belongs to the child of the "full" wife (recall Abraham, Ismael is never said to be the first-born of Abraham). In the nonbiblical documents reference is occasionally made to the first-born of a mother (cfr *ThWNT* VI 873, 877 fnt 30)—but here we are on nonbiblical soil.

the Baptizer, who also was the first child of his mother, it is not stressed that he was the first-born of Elizabeth (1:57).

These details, some of which do not agree with the normal Jewish legal language, show that the writer of Lk 2:4–7 was perfectly aware that he was dealing with a situation which is legally normal (Mary in Joseph's company as his normal wife) but factually abnormal in reference to Mary's pregnancy and childbirth (the child is "hers," he is "her first-born"). This is the framework which explains the description of Mary as "the one betrothed to Joseph": the writer of the sentence described Mary in this way (and not as wife) for the same reason that he stresses that she gave birth to "her" son and that this son is "her first-born"; namely, with the deliberate purpose of avoiding the suggestion that Mary was Joseph's wife in the comprehensive sense in which the term is normally understood, and that Jesus was Joseph's child.[141] And this was done in perfect agreement with, and in full dependence on, that which the same writer reported in Lk 1:26–38. If this understanding is rejected, the only alternative picture which emerges is this: a merely betrothed woman who is "with child," who is on a journey far away from home in the company of a man, and who, in some sort of emergency, gives birth to a child who is only "hers," who is "her first-born." And even in this alternative, the narrative does not offer the slighest indication that Joseph had begotten this child—rather the opposite is true.

The foregoing remarks make it difficult to maintain that nothing in Ch. 2 favors the virginal conception. An explanation has to be provided for the obvious departures from the normal Jewish language. Furthermore, in the rest of the chapter the writer refers to the "parents" of the child (2:27, 41, 43) or to "his father and mother" (2:33, 48); he fails to refer to Jesus

---

[141] Luke's wording shows the same concern which appears in some variant readings of Mt 1, 16: just in order to get around the notion that Joseph was Mary's husband these readings say that Joseph was betrothed to Mary or that Mary was betrothed to Joseph.

as "their" son or as "his" (Joseph's) son one single time. On the other hand, in 2:48f as important as the reference to Jesus's "father and mother" is his question "did you not know?" and his declaration that he had to be about the business of "his Father"—a declaration which is very revealing for our subject and which certainly discloses the understanding of the evangelist. Finally, even on the assumption that Ch. 2 offered nothing favoring the virginal conception, Ch. 1 stands and keeps all its value even for Ch. 2, for which it is a preparation (annunciation-conception is followed by birth). In fact, Ch. 2 does not contain any detail which is *against* the virginal conception —only a detail of this kind would be evidence that the perspectives of Ch. 1 and Ch. 2 are at variance; and this is not the case.

It has been pointed out, furthermore, that Lk is extremely careful in using the verb *gennan* (to beget) and *tiktein* (to give birth), especially in 2:6f. It is a "lexical phenomenon according to which when he refers to John's generation, the evangelist uses *gennan,* and when the generation of Jesus is presented he uses *tiktein*".[142] Several details show that "Luke avoided connecting *gennan* with Mary and Jesus." The only exception in Lk 1:35 was unavoidable since *tiktein* connotes the concept of birth, which does not apply at the time of 1:35. But the meaning of *gennan* in this passage is "to germinate, to be produced": that which will sprout, germinate, just as in Mt 1:20.

Summarizing, it can be said that—leaving the historical aspect aside for now—there can be little doubt about what the evangelist, or whoever wrote Lk 1-2, really means. An objective reading of Lk 1 and 2 leaves no other alternative than that the evangelist was convinced of the virginal conception of Jesus by Mary, and this is the message that he wanted to convey to

---

[142] These reflections have been recently proposed by Cernuda Antonio Vicent, 'El paralelismo de *genno y tikto* en Lk 1-2,' *Bib* 55 (1974) 260–264. The quotes are found in p. 260 and p. 262.

his readers. This conclusion derives from the very text of Lk, it has not to be taken from some other place, v.gr. from Mt, and to be read into Lk's narrative. No recourse to Mt is needed to discover what is explicit in Lk. Certainly, Lk does not provide any basis for saying that Joseph begot Jesus or that Jesus was his child. Also for Lk the only alternative to virginal conception is illegitimacy. The evangelist's understanding is further confirmed by his remark in 3:23 that Jesus was, "as was supposed," Joseph's son—he was believed to be, but the evangelist, this is the implication, knew that he was not. Another detail exclusive to Lk points in the same direction: in 11:27 the voice of the people (or the Christian tradition) blesses "the womb that bore you and the breasts that nursed you." Admittedly, when taken in isolation, the passage does not prove much. But when taken together with other elements in the New Testament it underscores the fact that it is the memory of Jesus' mother that survives in the Christian tradition. The fact remains that it is His mother and not His (human) father that is blessed.

It is generally conceded that the narrative in Mt is explicit in affirming the virginal conception of Jesus. This Gospel, therefore, does not pose any problem from this viewpoint. A few remarks will suffice.

The conviction of the evangelist comes to the fore very clearly in 1:16. In a genealogy where a man consistently begets the following man, the last man (Jesus) is not begotten by the man before the last (Joseph); the genealogical line is broken right at the end to which it was supposed to lead, in order to say that Joseph was just the husband of Mary of whom Jesus was born, thereby indicating that Joseph is not the father of Jesus.[143] In fact, what was begotten "in" Mary "is from the Holy Spirit" (1:20, 18).

Now, Mary appeared to be with child "after she had been betrothed (*mnesteutheises*) to Joseph." The Greek word is the same used by Lk in 1:27 and 2:5 but the tense is different. Mt uses the aorist (not perfect) participle, which keeps a relatively temporal value in reference to the moment when Mary happened to be with child; the temporal value being that Mary's pregnancy occurred *after* she had been betrothed, after the day of her betrothal, not before. This value points to the day when Mary became Joseph's *arusah* by entering the well identified marital status to which Lk 1:27 refers by a perfect participle.

In fact Mt also explicitly says that Mary's pregnancy occurred before Joseph took her to his house (1:20, 24), i.e. before the betrothed woman, after one year as a rule, went to live with her husband. It is not unlikely that the evangelist refers to the same event when he says that Mary happened to be with child "before they (Mary and Joseph) *came together*"

---

[143] Cfr Knoch Otto, 'Die Botschaft des Matthäusevangeliums über Empfängnis und Geburt Jesu vor dem Hintergrund der Christusverkündigung des Neuen Testaments,' *Zum Thema Jungfrauengeburt*, 45.

(*synelthein*), before they came to live together—unless one prefers for the Greek term its other usual meaning of coming together in marital relations. If the latter alternative is preferred the exclusion of Joseph as the child's father is all the more direct: Mary happened to be with child after their betrothal but before they had had marital relations.

It is obvious from this description that the "situational" stage of Jesus' conception is the same in Mt and in Lk. Mary is "betrothed" to Joseph, but she is not living with Joseph when she happens to be with child. Lk does not report explicitly that Mary, after the conception of Jesus, went to live with Joseph, but he takes for granted that this was the case when he presents Mary in Joseph's company on their journey to Bethlehem (2:5) and thereafter (2:16, 27, 33, 39, 41ff). On the contrary, it is Luke who stresses much more directly and strongly that Mary was a virgin when she conceived; Mt probably implies the same thing when he notes that Mary was a merely betrothed woman who was not living with her husband (which could be said of a re-betrothed widow also), whereas the quality of Mary's physical virginity when she became mother of Jesus has to be derived from the quotation of Isaiah (1:23). It is important to realize that Mt does not lay any emphasis on the virginal state of Mary when she conceives, whereas Luke emphasizes this state of Mary very forcefully, as we have seen. This realization is important because it shows that in Luke, even more than in Mt, Mary's conception appears as really "virginal." This is certainly not a detail which has to be taken, v.gr., from Mt and read into Lk's narrative, when it is much more explicit in Lk than in Mt. In this connection it is to be noticed that Mt calls Mary and Joseph "wife" and "husband" resp., (and refers to "divorce"), whereas Lk deliberately avoids this, even in 2:5.

From the very beginning, however, Mt is careful to note that it is "by the Holy Spirit" that Mary is with child (1:18); he insists on the same remark in v. 20. This, together with the fact of Joseph's anxieties[144] and the instruction given to him by the angel, stresses very strongly that Joseph is not the father of what "had been begotten in" Mary; it was begotten "by the Holy Spirit." Two other details have to be viewed in this perspective: the first is that, though Mary and Joseph are betrothed, she is "mother of Jesus" (v. 18), but Joseph is not his father, and this remains true throughout this narrative (2: 13f, 20, 21); the second is that, also for Mt, Mary gives birth to a child (v. 21)—but not "for Joseph," in spite of the reading in the old Syriac versions. Luke brings into relief the same concept when he stresses that the Spirit will overshadow and come upon the "virgin" who asks about the "how" of her maternity "since she is not going to know any man." It is obvious that the basic elements in this particular aspect of virginal conception are common to both Mt and Lk, in spite of variations in emphasis.

The conclusion is that Mt, or whoever wrote this narrative, also was convinced that Joseph was not the father of Jesus and that Mary was with child "by the Holy Spirit." The particular interest of Mt's narrative is that this writer explicitly and repeatedly emphasizes that Joseph is not the father of Jesus, even though he was Mary's "husband." One could say that the concern of Mt's narrative is not so much to show that the Holy Spirit was operative in Jesus' conception as to show that Joseph did not beget this child: though betrothed to Joseph, Mary is with child "before" they get together, before she is taken into Joseph's house; Joseph's anxiety shows that he had nothing to do with the situation; it is the Holy Spirit, not Joseph, who was

---

[144] Which are not to be taken as suspicion about Mary's faithfulness: cfr Germano J. M., 'Nova et vetera in pericopam de S. Joseph (Mt 1, 18–25),' *VD* 46 (1968) 351–362; Krämer Michael, 'Zwei Probleme aus Mt 1, 18–25 . . .,' *Salesianum* 26 (1964) 309–324; *id.*, 'Die Menschwerdung Jesu Christi nach Matthäus,' *Bib* 45 (1964) 1–34; Sicari Antonio A., 'Joseph Justus (Matteo 1, 19),' in *Saint Joseph durant les quinze premiers siècles de l'Eglise* (= *Cahiers de Joséphologie* 19 (1971) 62–83.

at work in Mary; the prophet spoke about a virgin with a child without a man; Joseph did not know his wife.[145]

This thrust of the passage is important because it renders the speculation about a theologoumenon impossible. If there is nothing of a virginal (supernatural) conception, then Jesus is an adulterous child—Joseph, the husband of his mother, is certainly not his father. In such an alternative the theologoumenon idea is just a cover-up for Mary's adulterous conduct and for Jesus' irregular origin.

A close look at Mt's account seems to indicate both a careful distinction in the use of *gennan/tiktein* and a certain agreement with Lk on this use. Above all, the three agreements between the virginal *tiktein* (give birth) of Lk and that in Mt cannot be more telling. In Lk 1:31 the angel announces to Mary "you will give birth to a son"; in Mt 1:21 he announces to Joseph "she will give birth to a son." Lk 2:7 discloses Mary's child-bearing, "she gave birth to her son"; the same thing in Mt 1:25, "she gave birth to a son." In Lk 2:11 the angel lets the shepherds know "a saviour was born (*tiktein*) to you"; the Magi of Mt 2:2 ask about "where the born king of the Jews is?" The other instances when *gennan* is used by Mt are explained by various motives operative in the different passages of the narrative. The passage of Mt 1:20f is particularly instructive: Mary does not *gennan,* she just gives birth (*tiktein*), and not *to* Joseph; on the other hand, something has sprouted or budded (*gennan* in passive) *in* her, but this is not by Joseph but by the Spirit.[146]

---

[145] Knoch O., 'Die Botschaft' 38: both in Mt and in Lk the message is: "that the father of the child is not Joseph but God himself through a miraculous intervention, Joseph and any other man being excluded."

[146] For further detail on this analysis see Cernuda Antonio Vicent, 'La dialéctica *genno-tikto* in Mt 1–2,' *Bib* 55 (1974) 408–417. The quote is found in p. 408.

SOME LITERARY AND THEOLOGICAL ASPECTS

Before Mt and Lk

Both evangelists, Mt and Lk, maintain and proclaim in their writings Jesus' virginal/supernatural conception by Mary. Historically, this fact shows that such was the belief of the evangelists and of (at least) their communities at the time they wrote their gospels somewhere about 80 A.D. But what was the situation concerning this particular issue before this time? The question is whether this belief was an old tradition—and to what extent—in the Christian community, whether it was believed in the entire community or only by some portions of it, whether the origins of such a belief can be traced back to historically reliable sources, whether—more in particular—the narratives in Mt and Lk are documents written by someone before them, whether the historical quality of these presumably pre-existing documents is reliable to any degree—and some other related issues.

An important remark, however, is that in view of all the difficulties involved, it is much easier and safer to deal with a document as it appears in Mt or in Lk than to try to discover and to reconstruct the origins and the evolution of the same document. Obviously such an attempt has by necessity to proceed through guesses and conjectures which render the tentative conclusions very shaky. It is obvious that the problems are of two kinds: historical and literary. But they are interwoven. We shall try to keep them separated to the extent that this is possible. The literary aspect will be considered first; then the historical.

The Redactional Problem.

The redactional problem, i.e. the possible origin of this narrative through different stages of composition by different hands, does not emerge in Mt where scholars agree that the composition of Mt 1–2 goes back to one and the same hand. But the question arises with particular interest in Lk. Among other views of lesser interest for us, it had been proposed and is maintained that Lk's infancy narratives are a composition of the evangelist on the basis of two previous written documents or sources: one covers chapter 1 and the other chapter 2, roughly.[147] The implication of this separation of the two sources is that the perspective in the first source is that Joseph was not the father of Jesus, whereas the second source contradicted this view and maintained that Jesus was the son of Joseph. Of course, no one knows where, when, by whom, the assumed sources were written.[148]

A closer look at the material itself may prove interesting and revealing from this particular point of view. It has been pointed out above that Ch. 2 continues the *chronological* sequence of the unfolding narrative started in Ch. 1. Now some other details can be brought into relief.

In the first place, cross references to Ch. 1 are easily detected in Ch. 2. In 2:5 the description of Mary's marital situation ("Mary the one betrothed to him," to Joseph) is a clear reference to 1:27, where the same Greek words are used. This detail, plus the mention of Mary's pregnancy, refers the reader back to the entire narrative of 1:26–38. Given the tendency of the writer to introduce his characters to the reader (see below), the fact that precisely Mary is not introduced in 2:5 is to be noticed—the reason for this omission being that Mary had been introduced in 1:27. The same thing applies to Joseph in 2:4 who is supposed to be known to the reader because of his presentation in 1:27. If in 2:4 it is repeated that he was of the house of David, it is because this detail explains why Joseph

---

[147] Cfr Leaney A. R. C., 'The Birth Narratives in St Luke and St Matthew,' *NTS* 8 (1961/2) 158–166, espec. p. 162.

[148] Cfr, however, Benoit P., 'L'Enfance de Jean-Baptiste'; Winter Paul, 'The Proto-Source of Luke I,' *NT* 1 (1956) 184–199, particularly p. 185f.

went to Bethlehem and not elsewhere. Concerning Nazareth
this is how it is presented in 1:26: the angel "goes to a town
in Galilee the name of which is Nazareth"; on the contrary, in
2:4 Joseph comes "from Galilee out of the town of Nazareth."
The comparison shows that in 2:4 Nazareth is already known
to the reader, and this is why it is not said that it is "a town
of Galilee" (this is known in 2:4) and why the explanation
"the name of which" is missing, whereas immediately afterwards (in 2:4) the author refers to the town of David in Judea
"which is called Bethlehem," in perfect agreement with the
literary procedure followed in 1:26 for Nazareth. In other
words, the reference to Nazareth in 2:4 presupposes the description of this town in 1:26.

In the passage of 2:21 which reports when Jesus was given
his name, the reference to 1:31 is unmistakable—to the point
that the Greek expressions used are the same, including the
reference to the angel of the annunciation, the redundant *en
gastri* (1:31) -*en te koilia* (2:21) and the semitic redundance in
kalein to onoma autou (cfr difference in 1:60f, 59). Obviously the reference to the angel, to the naming of the child by him,
and to the time "before the child was conceived in the womb"
is clear evidence that 2:21 could not be written unless the entire narrative of the annunciation had preceded in the same
document. On the other hand the circumcision and the naming
of Jesus in 2:21 is, in the literary and chronological design of
the writer, the counterpart of the corresponding episode of
John's story in 1:59–63. The heavily semitic character of each
and of all the clauses in 2:21 offers no grounds for the view
that the verse is an editorial creation of Luke, on the assumption that he uses written sources.

The quotation from Is 42:6 etc. in Lk 2:31 corresponds, no
doubt, to the prophets who foretold the coming of the Saviour
in 1:70, particularly when one realizes that in the same song
of Zachariah in 1:79 a reference to the messianic light is found
which goes back to Is 9:1 and 42:7. In 2:49, 50 Jesus' expres-

sion "did you not know" and his reference to God as "my Father," in the mind of the writer is a reminder to the reader of the annunciation narrative.

Both in Ch. 1 and in Ch. 2 the characters are introduced to the reader the first time they come on the stage. In Ch. 1 we find the presentation of Zachariah and Elizabeth (1:5ff), that of Mary and Joseph (1:27) and, in a certain sense, that of John (1:80). In Ch. 2 we find the introduction of Symeon (2:25), that of Anne (2:36) and, we may say, that of Jesus (2:40, 55).

Besides this literary feature (not found in Mt 1–2) common to both chapters, it is particularly striking that these introductions offer specific patterns in both chapters for the introduction of men, for the introduction of women and for that of children, to the point that the expressions themselves are identical. In 2:25 the reference is to "a man of the name (*ho onoma*) of Symeon"; in 1:27 the reference is to "a husband of the name (*ho onoma*) of Joseph." In 2:25 Symeon is "just and pious"; in 1:6 Zachariah and his wife were "just"—and kept God's commandments, which is an expansion of "pious." In 2:36 Anne is "a daughter of Phanuel . . . she was advanced in years"; but in 1:5 Elizabeth also was "of the daughters of Aaron" and both she and her husband "were advanced in their years" (1:7 and, again, in 1:18 Elizabeth "was advanced in her years"). At this point we also may notice in both chapters the tendency to relate individuals to their ancestry: in 2:36 Anne is "of the tribe of Asser"; in Ch. 1:5 Zachariah is of the priestly "class of Abijah," and Joseph is "of the house of David" (1:27). The description of Jesus in 2:40 and that of John in 1:80 are identical: in 2:40 (Jesus) "the child was growing up and was gaining strength filled with wisdom"; in 1:80 (John) "the child was growing up and was gaining strength of spirit." Furthermore, "the grace of God was upon him" upon Jesus (2:40; cfr 2:52); in 1:66 "the hand of the Lord was upon him," with John. It can be added that social relationships are expressed according to a common pattern in both chapters: 2:44 refers to *hoi syggeneis kai hoi gnostoi;* and 1:58 refers to *hoi periokoi kai syggeneis;* in 1:36 the reference is to *he syggeneis* (cfr 1:61).

The same expression and the same grammatical construction are used in both chapters for chronological indications. In 2:1 the indication is "it happened in those days"; and in 1:5 the indication is "it happened in the days of Herod," just as in 1:39 reference is made to "in these days" (as for *egeneto de* in 2:1, 6 see 1:8). A different chronological indication appears in 2:6: "the days were completed for her (Mary) to give birth" (*tou tekein auten*); but also in 1:57 "the time was completed for her (Elizabeth) to give birth" (*tou tekein auten*)— in both places the characteristic construction (*tou* and infinitive) is found which is used again in 2:21: "the eight days were completed to circumcise" (*tou peritemein*), whereas in 1:23 "the days of (gen.) his liturgical service were completed" (cfr also 2:22).

The concept of motion can be expressed in the same way in both chapters: *poreuesthai eis* (to travel to) is found in 2:3, 41, but it is found also in 1:39; the idea of return to some place is expressed by *hypostrephein eis* in 2:43, 45, but the same terms are found in 1:56 (cfr in 2:39 *epistrephein* with a variant reading); *hypostrephein* without *eis* appears in 2:20.

Geographical descriptions are made in both chapters much according to the same pattern: a town is mentioned together with the province or district to which the town (even in 1:39) belongs; the province is not described any further, but the town, when mentioned for the first time, is identified by the name, if known: a town "called Nazareth, Bethlehem." This pattern is found not only in 2:4 but also in 1:26. It can be added that every definite place (even in 2:3), however small, is a "town" (*polis*) in both chapters: Nazareth is a town both in 1:26 and in 2:4, 39, and the place where Zachariah lived is a town also (1:39); Bethlehem also is a town (2:4, 11), whereas it is a "village" in Jn 7:42 (cfr Mt 2:6).

There are, furthermore, several more or less characteristic expressions which are found throughout the entire narrative, both in Ch. 1 and in Ch. 2.[149] Here are some: an angel of the Lord (2:8; 1:11); *evaggelizasthai* (*hymin* 2; 10; *soi* 1; 19; the meaning is not genuinely Christian in either case); *chara estai* (*panti* 2:10; *soi* 1:14); *rhema*, with the meaning of "thing" or fact, in 2:15 and in 1:65, as well as in 2:19, 51b where the entire sentences correspond to 1:65b-66a (cfr 2:17, 50); *pantes ethaumasan* (all were surprised) is found both in 2:18 and 1:63; if the shepherds go to Bethlehem *speusantes* (2:16), so Mary goes to Elizabeth *meta spoudes* (1:39); *lalein pros* is found both in 2:15, 18, 20 and in 1:19, 55 (with dative, it is also found in 2:17, 38, 50 and in 1:22, 45); the expression "his name was called Jesus" in 2:21, besides being a cross-reference to 1:31, has an equivalence in the similar expression "his name, in (C *prima manus* and D) will be called John" (cfr the difference in 1:59); *eulogein ton theon* can be read in 2:28 and in 1:64 (cfr 1:42, 68) in the same sense that Mary and the fruit of her womb are declared *eulogemenoi* by Elizabeth in 1:42; *kata to ethos* (*tes heortes*) is found in 2:42 (cfr 2:27) but also (*tes hierateias*) in 1:9, whereas in the rest of the New Testament it is found only in Lk 22:39 (in LXX, only in 2 Macc 11:25 and Dan Bel 15, Theod); the construction *en to hypostrephein autous* in 2:43 has its equivalent in *en to hierateuein auton* in 1:8; as for the rather infrequent *dioti* in 2:7, cfr 1:13; as for *kai sou de* in 2:34, cfr 1:76.

Some other terms reflect the same theological concern in both chapters: Anne talked to those who were longing for the *lytrosis* of Jerusalem (2:38), and Zachariah praises God precisely because He "brought about *lytrosis*[150] for his people"

---

[149] Many of these expressions and other details mentioned before are considered as "Lukanisms" by Benoit P., 'L'Enfance de Jean Baptiste,' 170–176; George A., 'Le parallèle,' 149–168.

[150] Benoit P., *ibid.* 183, with others, maintains that the Greek wording for

(1:68); though the expressions are different, the concept of
lytrosis appears when Symeon is longing for the *paraclesis*
of Israel (2:25), when his eyes have seen *to soterion* of God
(2:30) or when Mary proclaims that God *antelabeto* (came to
the help of) Israel (1:54); the concept of "joy" both in 2:10
and 1:13 (28) has already been pointed out. This finding
is corroborated by the fact that the predominant theological
concept in the narrative—God's salvation is already here—
goes through both Ch. 1 and Ch. 2: in chapter 1 this concept
is the theme of Mary's and Zachariah's songs, as well as the
theme indicated by the effects of Mary's presence and by the
statements of Elizabeth in the visitation narrative (1:41–45);
in chapter 2 this concept is the subject of Symeon's song and
of Anne's talks "about the child" to everyone who was "longing
for the redemption" of Israel, as well as of her "praises of
God" when she met the child (2:38)—besides the "good news"
proclaimed by the angel, namely, the savior was born "today"
(2:11), he is already here.[151]

Some psychological reactions in the people, captured in these
narratives, are the same in both chapters, and are described in
very similar terms. The clearest instance is 2:17–19 compared
to 1:63. In the former passage as the shepherds talked about
the apparition and message of the angels "all those who heard
were surprised about the things the shepherds told them, but
Mary was treasuring up all these things and was pondering
them in her heart" (cfr 2:51). In the latter, "all were surprised" at the happenings at John's birth and circumcision,
"and throughout the hill country of Judah all these things were
talked about and all those who heard them kept them in mind,
thinking: What will this child be?"

The foregoing analysis shows that, at the present level, it

---

this expression does not reflect a Hebrew original—the suggestion being that
it is Luke's wording.

[151] Laurentin René, 'Traces d'allusions étymologiques en Luc 1–2,' *Bib*
37 (1956) 44ff, finds references to the name "Jesus" in both ch. 1 and 2—
on the assumption of the Hebrew original.

is not easy to dissociate chapters 1 and 2 as independent and unrelated sources. One and the same design goes through both of them. The data in Ch. 1 are referred to in Ch. 2, and in some instances Ch. 2 takes for granted that chapter 1 has preceded. The literary and stylistic features are the same in both chapters, and so are the theological concerns, some characteristic expressions and psychological remarks. To say that a second hand (i.e. Luke) equalized two independent documents as they were integrated into one narrative is not tenable. The theological tendency mentioned above is the essence of the entire narrative and particularly of the songs, in both chapters. The description of characters, which in both chapters reveals the same literary tendency and the same stylistic features, is not an additional retouch but belongs to the very body of the narrative. The same thing has to be said concerning some chronological indications like "the days were completed" (for her to give birth, 1:57; 2:5; to circumcise, 2:21; in the liturgical service, 1:23; for purification, 2:22) in a narrative which follows a chronological sequence (cfr 1:24, 26, 36, 56, 57, 59, 80; 2:6, 21, 22, 39, 40, 42). The geographical indications concerning Nazareth and Bethlehem also belong to the very basics of this particular narrative which is concerned with the origins of "Christ" (notice that the geographical accuracy is missing in the case of John).

Some other expressions have been pointed out which are found in both chapters. It is unlikely that they come from an "equalizing" hand. For one thing, it would be rather unusual that a second hand went so deeply into his written source or was so scrupulous in his equalizing work, as to balance his retouches. It is much more obvious to admit that such was the writing habit of one and the same author. For another, if someone tries to press the aspect of Lukanisms, it is easier to admit that either Luke wrote the whole narrative on the basis of some oral tradition, or that he translated a semitic original according to his own personal style.

Beyond the literary analysis, there are some other considerations. It is unthinkable that the document which contained the annunciation to Mary did not contain the birth of Jesus.[152] One wonders on what rational grounds could it be explained that a "Christian" who undertakes to report the origins of the man he worships, describes at considerable length how this man was conceived and then he does not report that this man was born. This would be all the more strange since, concerning John, the same document allegedly reports his conception and his birth. Theoretically it could be said that the same document contained both the conception and the birth of Jesus but that Luke preferred to take the annunciation from one document and the birth from another. Such arbitrariness, however, does not seem to be very rational, particularly if the second document displayed a tendency contrary to the first—and, at any rate, there is no evidence for such an assumption.

All considerations, of various orders, lead to the conclusion that at the basis of Lk 1–2 we have a single document which reported John's and Jesus' miraculous conceptions, births and circumcisions, together with other episodes related to them.

Admittedly, the episodes of Jesus' presentation in the temple (2:22–24), of Symeon's and Anne's encounter with the child (2:25–38) and of Jesus' discussion with the "doctors" in Jerusalem have no correspondence in John's stories. But this only underscores the fact that the author intended to write about Jesus (not about someone else), and that it is in Jesus' history that he is interested. He is, however, the same author who wrote the rest of these narratives, since we have seen that in these units the same theological, literary and stylistic features are present as in the rest of Ch. 1 and Ch. 2.

The literary unit of chapters 1 and 2 in Luke leads to a con-

---

[152] Schürmann Heinz, 'Aufbau, Eigenart und Geschichtswert der Vorgeschichte von Lukas 1–2,' BiKi 21 (1966) 106, notes that "the central point of this series of narratives is no doubt the episode of Jesus' birth in 2, 1–20 . . ."

clusion that is doctrinal in character. There is no evidence to support the view that behind the narratives in Lk 1 and 2 there are two (or more) written sources of conflicting tendencies concerning the virginal conception of Jesus. The same hand who wrote chapter 2 wrote chapter 1 also.

The existing literary evidence provides no grounds to see in chapter 1 a document stressing the virginal conception and in Ch. 2 a different document maintaining that Joseph was the physical father of Jesus. Admittedly, it is only in chapter 2 that the author relates Joseph to Jesus as "his father" several times, or to Mary and Joseph as "his parents." But, as pointed out above, the author of Ch. 2 never relates Jesus to Joseph as "his" child, or to Joseph and Mary as "their" child. This can be compared with Mt's accuracy who always speaks of "the child and his mother" (2:11, 13, 14, 21), but never to Joseph's child or to "their" child. It is important to notice that the Gospel narrative refers to "his" father and parents only *after* Jesus' birth when the full reality of a family emerged in which a child is in relationship to a man and to a woman united in a marital life, and when the social concept of family and its terminology could be used in common language not overconscious of precision.

But even in the case that one would admit an independent source in Lk 2 the expressions "his father, his parents" does not contradict the point of view expressed in Lk 1. One wonders why the remark in Lk 3:23 that Jesus "was believed to be" Joseph's son should apply to what follows in the main body of the Gospel only, and not to what goes before also, i.e. to the infancy narratives. When Luke in 4:22 (cfr Mat 13:55; Jn 6:42) bears witness that public opinion considered Jesus as "Joseph's son" as He began His ministry, he implicitly says that this was the case before Jesus' ministry also. One wonders why the narratives in Ch. 2 should not bear witness to the same public opinion ever since Jesus was born within a family structure. This applies even when Mary is reported as saying that "your father and I were looking for you" (Lk 2:48); in this case the report would express the views of the reporter, not necessarily those of Mary.[153] Such a perspective certainly enhances Luke's respect for his sources and, as a result and to that extent, his reliability as a historian.

The evangelist who is careful to exclude the normal process of generation in the case of Jesus up to 2:21, did not think he was contradicting his views as he brings into this narrative these episodes which refer to Jesus' "father" or "parents," whatever the popular opinion of any previous report. He judged that these statements were reconcilable with this doctrine of the virginal conception, and there is no reason why we also should not be able to reconcile them.

Literary Paternity

A different problem is whether this literary unit in Lk 1–2 was put in writing by Luke himself for the *first* time, or whether he already found it in a written source. In the case of a possible written source a further question arises: what was the original language of the document? Hebrew or Aramaic? An original in Greek or a Greek translation previous to Luke himself has never been a serious alternative. Obviously, these questions intend to discover the pre-history of the Lukan narrative. Important though they are for the historical origins of the belief in Jesus' virginal conception, it is clear for everyone to see that we move into a field of conjecture and speculation. The conflicting answers put forward bear out this remark.

Everyone agrees that in its present form the document betrays

---

153 Yersel B. M. F. van, 'The Finding of Jesus in the Temple,' *NT* 4 (1961) 161–173, is of the view that Lk 2, 41–51a is an independent story that before "was part of the tradition before the primitive church had become conscious of Jesus' virgin birth and its implications" (p. 164) . . . (it is probable) "that Luke II 41–51a in its paradigmatic form belongs to a primitive stage of the tradition, which, also according to Bultmann and Dibelius, provides us with the most reliable information about Jesus that can be derived from the synoptic gospels" (p. 172f).

the hand of Luke at almost every sentence (except for the hymns). Evidence for this are the linguistic and stylistic remarks made by Benoit and George.[154] Everyone agrees, furthermore, that these narratives betray a Jewish-Palestinian background, both in historical details (cfr v. gr. Lk 1:8–10, 21, 29) and in literary expression.[155] This second agreement is important for the historical origin of the faith in the virginal conception. The agreements, however, end there.

P. Winter has argued very strongly that the narrative in Lk 1–2 was originally written in Hebrew.[156] Furthermore, in another paper[157] he maintains without hesitancy that these narratives were written by Jewish authors in Palestine. Lk 1 and 2

could not be written by anyone but a person, or persons rooted in Jewish social traditions, religious custom, and general folklore, and acquainted with the topographic features of the surroundings in which the story is set . . . the author or authors, whose literary work with little changes we still possess in Luke I, II, were Jews who were living in Palestine in a Jewish community well before the start of the armed conflict with Rome, and who shared in that community's social conventions and held its general outlook on life (p. 159f).

In particular he analyzes Lk 1:5, 9f, 19, 58; 2:8, 37. No pagan, he maintains, could know several details in these narratives, first of all these dealing with the temple liturgy (1:10, 21), "as no gentile was, under penalty of death, permitted to enter even the second outer court in front of the sanctuary"[158]—in point of

---

[154] Benoit P., 'L'Enfance'; George A., 'Le parallèle.'

[155] Cfr, v. gr., Schürmann H., 'Aufbau,' 110.

[156] Winter P., 'Some Observations on the language in the Birth and Infancy Stories of the Third Gospel,' *NTS* 1 (1954/5) 111–121. A Hebrew (not Aramaic) original in some form (written or oral) is the view maintained by most scholars: cfr Laurentin R., 'Le problème du substrat hébreu de Luc 1–2,' *Bib* 37 (1956) 449–456; *id.*, 'Traces d'allusions,' 449.

[157] Winter P., 'The Cultural Background of the Narrative in Luke I and II,' *JQR* 45 (1954/5) 159–167; 230–242. A rather peculiar view is expressed by *id.*, 'The Proto-Source of Luke I.'

[158] 'The Cultural Background,' 236.

fact, "a gentile author writing at a time when the Temple no longer stood could not have known this."[159]

Against Winter and others, Benoit contends that the narrative in Lk 1 and 2 was written by Luke himself as the many "Lukanisms" show. The abundant and obvious "Hebraisms" are explained by Benoit by a set design in Luke to imitate the sacred language of the Septuagint; what we have in Luke are "Septuagintisms" rather than Hebraisms. Benoit's evidence is really impressive, and cannot be easily dismissed.

As for me, I find it more likely and more simple that Luke himself wrote here in a style voluntarily biblical, full of almost literal reminiscences of the LXX—though showing the effects of his style, so personal, in many passages.[160]

Benoit is perfectly aware that the historical and chronological details which suggest to Winter a Jewish authorship, reflect a sound tradition and cannot be explained by a literary imitation of the LXX. But Benoit sees no need to resort to a source written by any Jewish author. Those details are explained by Benoit on the basis of an authentic, i.e. solidly grounded, *oral* tradition which came down to Luke.

The elements which cannot be reduced to merely literary imitations are the otherwise pretty vague circumstances of time and place: in the temple of Jerusalem, at Herod's time; then the personages Zacharijah and Elizabeth of whom one belongs to the class of Abijah, the other to the daughters of Aaron . . . These details must derive from an historical tradition . . . One gets the feeling that he is dealing with good information; but this can be sufficiently explained by an oral tradition coming from Jewish-Christian circles of Jerusalem.[161]

159 *Ibid.*, 167.
160 Benoit P., 'L'Enfance,' 175.
161 *Ibid.*, 178.

The literary evidence provided by Benoit cannot be easily dismissed. The historical considerations stressed by Winter stand even in Benoit's opinion: the historical background goes back to a Jewish Palestinian tradition acquainted with places, usages, religious practices, language, of a community living in Palestine. Whether this historical background came to Luke in a written document or through an oral tradition is hard to tell; a clear decision on this issue will probably never be reached. At any rate, there is widespread agreement that it was Luke who gave the final form to the infancy narrative we read in his Gospel, and that, on account of their historical and local setting, these episodes go back to some time before Luke.

The semitic color as well as the Palestinian setting is very prominent in the narratives of Matthew also. And that is why it is generally admitted that the infancy stories of Mt go back to a Jewish source too.

The considerations under the foregoing headings have some relevance for the historical aspect of the belief in Jesus' virginal conception. The fact that the narratives in Mt and Lk are independent of each other is evidence that the belief in the virginal conception is not an invention of either evangelist nor is it the invention of either of the communities represented by these evangelists. In geographical terms this means that there is historical evidence that the doctrine of the virginal conception was known and believed in at least two unrelated and independent communities, probably located far apart. The fact that the evidence is restricted to two communities only, does not imply that the doctrine mentioned was unknown in other communities. The assumption would rather be the opposite, precisely because two *unrelated* communities believe the same thing —the possible implication being that such a doctrine was at least known in other communities, if it was not the common Christian belief.[162]

In chronological terms the agreement between Mt and Lk means that the belief in the virginal conception goes back to an origin from which their immediate source derived, and, as a result, to a time earlier than the composition of their Gospels.[163] Admittedly, there is no precise indication by which to set a precise date for the original source. Still, it can be noticed that in both geographical and chronological terms the fact that the

[162] It is generally admitted that Mt represents a semitic (Jewish-Christian) community, though it is not easy to pinpoint a place for this community. Likewise it is generally agreed that Lk represents some community in the Greco-Roman world. But, is there any evidence to link or to relate the Gospel of Luke to some individual community?

[163] Cfr Danieli G., 'A proposito delle origini della tradizione sinottica sulla concezione verginale,' *Dth* 72 (1969) 317ff: "Let us remain . . . between 30 and 50/60 nearly. During this time . . . the tradition about the virginal conception must have appeared in the Church and have been accepted, practically unopposed."

infancy narratives and, therefore, the belief in the virginal conception derive from a Jewish Palestinian community is very important. In the first place, this is a third community where the doctrine we discuss was held. Moreover, it relates the belief in this doctrine to the geographical area where all other evangelic records come from, where this and other evangelic episodes unfolded and where the people involved in this and other episodes lived, even after the episodes took place; it is from this area also that the first witnesses to the Christian faith went forth.

The Jewish Palestinian background of the infancy narratives is important chronologically also—which emerges with particular clarity in Lk. The records preserved in the third Gospel refer to a Jewish priest and to a priestly family (Abijah) in *active* office (1:5); Lk refers to an *actual* liturgical service *in the temple,* of which service he gives a fairly accurate description (1:9f, 21, 23); the evangelist reports the presence of Jesus, Mary and Joseph in the Jewish temple of Jerusalem when Jesus is "presented to the Lord," where Mary complies with the Jewish prescriptions and actually offers a sacrifice (2:22–24), where pious Jews like Symeon and Anne go and pray (2:27–37); not only this, but the entire family is presented as visiting the temple in Jerusalem "every year" (2:40); again, it is in the temple that the rabbis discuss religious matters (as Jesus does later on: Lk 19:47; 21:37, etc.) and that Jesus was found. This setting shows that these narratives could not be fabricated at any time after the destruction of the Jewish temple; they derive from a time when the temple was still standing as the center of the Jewish worship and piety. The narratives, therefore, go back to some time before 70 A.D.— and so does the belief in the virginal conception. The same thing can be said of Mt, as the "high priest and scribes *of the people"* are mentioned in 2:4. It can be recalled that Mk was written some time before 70 A.D. How much before 70 should these narratives be placed, is for everyone to guess. There is no clear indication to establish any particular date to any degree of accuracy.

This much, however, can be added. The traditions reported by Mt and Lk are already considerably different in contents and, particularly, in presentation. As in the case of the gospel tradition, this is evidence that some time has gone by since these narratives came to exist for the first time until they reached the evangelists. This is a conclusion which is supported by the primitive character of the theological concepts in these accounts (see below). Or should it be admitted that the narratives of Lk and Mt originated in two different communities of Palestine? This alternative not only would call for a certain span of time between these original communities and the gospels, but it would prove both that even before Mt and Lk several communities shared the same belief in the virgin birth and that the common fontal origin of the information is still further behind those original communities.

Another aspect of the historical problem is the *historicity* or historical value of these narratives. In this regard, a preliminary remark is that the general setting of the narratives is certainly historically reliable as it is grounded on facts firmly established by other sources. Luke refers to Herod, the king of Judah, who is certainly a historical figure; even more importantly, he says that the events he is setting out to write took place in Herod's time, which is absolutely true. The reference to different "orders" and "terms of service" among the Jewish priests is a solid datum. The reference to the family of Abijah as one of the orders of priests is historically correct. The rite of offering the incense inside the temple as the people were praying outside, is well established by other sources also.[164] The marital

---

[164] Winter P., 'The Cultural Background,' 167: "When therefore Lk I, 9 records that the lot to burn incense in the Temple had fallen to Zekharyah, this detail is in exact correspondence with what is known of the procedure and organization of the Temple service at that time. Without access to Jewish sources, a gentile author writing at a time when the Temple no longer stood could not have known this."

status of Mary as "a virgin betrothed to a man" is well attested in the Jewish law of the time. The circumcision of a boy eight days after his birth (Lk 1:59; 2:21) was the law (Lev 12:3) and the practice (Phil 3:5) of the time.[165] The reference in 2:8 to shepherds taking turns in watching their flocks at night, is considered as in perfect agreement with reality by P. Winter.

The circumstances of Christ's birth in a *katalyma* (sort of lodging) where there was no better place than a manger to lay the child seems to correspond to factual situations.[166] In spite of the problems that the census in Lk 2:1–4 poses, in general it certainly agrees with what is known in this regard about that time.[167] That Augustus' rule was contemporaneous with Herod's (1:4) is historically sound also. The presence of the teachers in the temple area (Lk 2:46) is not denied by Christ's practice of teaching there (Jn 8:2; 10:23; cfr Acts 5:12). The pilgrimage to Jerusalem by Passover (Lk 2:41), was a normal practice among the pious Jews (cfr Jn 11:55; 12:20).

In his turn, the writer of Mt 1:19 is on solid historical grounds in reference to Mary's marital status and nuptial customs, as well as when he speaks of Joseph thinking about "divorcing" his betrothed wife. He also refers to Herod under whose rule Jesus was born (2:1ff). The important element here, however, is that the author characterizes Herod by some salient traits which are well known from other sources: his suspicion of threats against his throne (2:3ff), and his cruelty (2:13, 16). It is historically true also that Herod died just a few years after Jesus' birth (2:19); as it is historically true

---

[165] *Id., ibid.* 238: "This feature of the narrative only needs to be compared with IV Ezra 9, 45 to disclose the author's intimate knowledge of Jewish custom and folklore. It is one further instance on which it may be shown that not only the diction in Lk I, II is Hebraic, but that the background of the story is genuinely Jewish. The familiarity of the author with Jewish life and custom is beyond doubt."

[166] Cfr Benoit P., 'Non erat eis locus in Diversorio (Lc 2, 7),' *Mélanges . . . Rigaux*, 173–186.

[167] Cfr Sherwin-White, A. N. *Roman Society and Roman Law in the New Testament* (Oxford, 1963) 168ff.

that Herod was succeeded by his son Archelaus, and that Archelaus succeeded Herod in the rule of Judah *only,* and not, v. gr., in the rule of Galilee—this is the reason why Joseph goes to Nazareth in Galilee as he was afraid to go to Judah (2:22), since, according to historical records again, Archelaus was as cruel as his father.

These details show that there is a diffused historical dimension to the infancy narratives. The chronological agreement between Mt and Lk (Herod-Archelaus-Augustus) strengthens such a dimension. This realization certainly does not favor the presumption of non-historicity in these narratives.

History and Exotic Literature

The main problem concerning historicity, however, arises from the literary character of these narratives. The question is whether the literary genre used in these narratives is compatible with historicity to any degree. In our particular discussion about the virginal conception the question is whether, given the peculiar literary genre of these narratives, the original author or authors (in Mt and Lk) of these narratives intended to present such a belief as an historical fact—regardless of the fact that Mt and Lk might have understood their sources in historical terms.

It is obvious, in fact, that in these narratives the miraculous element is more abundant than in the rest of the Gospel narratives themselves. Angels convey messages to the fathers and mothers of the boys to be born, they give instructions through dreams about what is to be done, and appear in heavenly radiance announcing the birth of a boy and singing the praises of the Lord. The visitation of a mother supernaturally influences the other mother and the child in her womb. The Spirit guides pious people to meet and disclose the saving meaning of the newly-born child. An infant prodigy probes and defies the scholarship of learned doctors; foreigners come to know about the child's birth, by means of a peculiar star they can distinguish from the others, and set out on their way to see the child as the star leads them, etc. This certainly does not happen every day. Besides, old and sterile parents beget a child, a virgin becomes a mother without man's intervention.

There is more. This kind of religious literature about births of important persons, in which the miraculous is profusely interspersed, is a well established literary genre used in Jewish writings anterior and contemporary to the New Testament,[168] besides some cases of miraculous births or of miraculous, divine interventions to save a child's life that are known to the Old Testament also. Moses, Isaac, Jacob-Esau, Samson, Samuel should be mentioned in this connection. On the other hand, it is obvious that the sources of both Mt and Lk sometimes compose their narratives with deliberate reference to these comparable cases of the Old Testament, and perhaps to some extrabiblical traditions which came down to us in writing and which could have been known to them in some form (written or oral). At any rate, the infancy narratives in Mt and Lk present the same literary characteristics of this sort of Jewish literature.

Whether this literary genre should be defined as *midrash, haggadah* or *pesher* is irrelevant at this moment[169]—it is merely a question of semantics. What is important is the substance and the message of this form of writing. There can be little doubt that in many cases in the Jewish literature the episodes cannot be grounded on reliable information. It is obvious that around the times of the New Testament and after, no information about Noah, Abraham, Isaac, etc. was available except that contained in the Old Testament. Still, the Jewish religious literature under discussion could describe events concerning

[168] Cfr Perrot Charles, 'Les Récits d'enfance dans la Haggada antérieure au II⁰ siècle de notre ère,' *RechSR* 55 (1967) 481–518.

[169] Cfr Graystone G., *Virgin of all Virgins,* 59–61; Schürmann H., 'Aufbau,' 108f; Schneider G., 'Jesu geistgewirkte Empfängnis' 108; Wright Addison G., *The Literary Genre Midrash* (Staten Island, 1967) esp. p. 139ff (also in *CBQ* 28 (1966) 105–138; 417–457).

their birth and early years with great detail of miraculous or prodigious happenings. It is worth noticing, furthermore, that only prominent individuals in the Salvation History are the subject of these extraordinary births, etc. Obviously, the purpose of these peculiar narratives is to stress the importance of those individuals in the saving plan of God, who displays a particular providence in their regard.

It is the external agreement between this Jewish literature and the infancy narratives in Mt and Lk that poses the problem of historicity in the latter in burning terms—though it is to be noticed that Lk is much more sober and discreet than Mt. In principle, however, one can say that historicity is not incompatible with any literary genre. Conversely, there is no literary genre that by its own nature can ever contain and convey historical information, even in the case that it is not ordinarily used to write history. In this regard, a lot depends on the aims of a particular author and on the relationship existing between a given author and the facts he reports. On the other hand, an author can choose a given literary genre to present the historical facts he reports in a particular light, in order not to offer *bruta facta* only but also their meaning and significance.

A basic difference between the infancy narratives in the Gospels and the Jewish religious literature we are referring to, is that the infancy narratives are, chronologically, very close to the subject they deal with. The Jewish literature deals with individuals of the early times of the Old Testament, such as Noah, Samuel, Elijah, who lived centuries and millenia before this religious literature was written. On the contrary, the Gospel infancy narratives, that certainly go back to some time before 70 A.D., deal with Jesus of Nazareth who lived just a few decades earlier. Many persons directly acquainted with Jesus and with his history were still alive, no doubt, when these narratives came to exist. This certainly makes a great difference from the viewpoint of historicity. The authors of the Gospel infancy narratives could be witnesses to the episodes they report, and they could be reporting real facts, about the existence of which they entertained no doubts; even though they report them in such a way that sometimes it is difficult for us to reconstruct the nature and the proportions of the events to which they refer. The fact itself could have been of very modest proportions and natural in character; but the reporter tries, not to take note of the fact itself, but to convey its great theological significance to his reader, and that is why he resorts to particular literary methods to achieve this purpose. In the process, however, the theological radiance has transfigured the fact itself, the historical and concrete identity of which will be difficult to recover.

The answer to the problem, therefore, is not to deny *a priori* any historical dimension to this literary genre wherever it is used and, more particularly, to the infancy narratives in the Gospels, for this can be done only at the risk of throwing out the baby with the bath water. The only correct procedure is to analyze very thoroughly the various cases and to determine the degree of historical truth in each episode—and to acknowledge, wherever necessary, the limitations of the information and of the methods at our disposal in every attempt to reconstruct the past.

As pointed out above, the general framework of the first two chapters in both Mt and Lk shows that there is a historical dimension to their infancy narratives. This historical dimension, however, goes beyond the general (and external) framework. In point of fact, these narratives deal with Jesus, Mary and Joseph, who are persons perfectly identifiable at this period of history by sources other than the infancy narratives. The same thing applies to the case of John the Baptizer. The birth of Jesus in Bethlehem is well established on very early post-biblical evidence.[170] That Jesus and Mary are related as son and mother rests on the basis of the entire Christian records

---

[170] Recall the profanation of the place by Hadrian.

outside these narratives. The same tradition is witness to the fact that Jesus and Joseph (and Mary) were related to each other within a family structure. That Jesus was raised and lived in Nazareth as in "his home town" is commonplace in the fourfold Gospel tradition of Christ's ministry; and that Nazareth is in Galilee is perfectly correct. That Bethlehem was associated with David and his family is a solid datum of Old Testament history; as it is geographically true that Nazareth is in Galilee. The distinction itself between Judea and Galilee is accurate. Particularly striking is that in Mt 1:22f the text of Is 7:14 is quoted *in extenso* as a sort of scriptural evidence of the episode; now in Is 7:14 it says that the name of the "virgin's" child is Emmanuel—but, oddly enough, Mary's child is called Jesus, as historical truth demanded. That a boy went on pilgrimage to Jersalem when he was 12 (Lk 2:42) is in perfect agreement with the customary law of the time.[171] The assumption that the missing Jesus could be in the travelling group of pilgrims (Lk 2:43f) also corresponds to the usages of the time.[172] The piece of information that a "child" was living in desert areas (Lk 1:80) is so strange that its oddness is the evidence of its reliability. At any rate, the existence of Jewish religious communities like that of Qumran in the desert of Judea provides a framework which adds to the historical soundness of the Gospel information. This framework offers a more ready explanation, in historical terms, of the fact that the child was "gaining in fortitude of spirit." The perspective of a "child raised in the desert" (cfr 3:2) far from denying, supports the information that his parents were old. Benoit[173] points out that John the Baptizer's priestly origin must be historically true, precisely because there is nothing in his subsequent life which would suggest such an origin. This is an indication that

---

[171] Strack H.-Billerbeck P., *Kommentar zum NT* II, 144ff.
[172] *Ibid.,* 149.
[173] Benoit P., 'L'Enfance,' 178. He also points out that Zachariah's dumbness must have been real, since the biblical tradition does not know of any "sign" which is a punishment.

the information that John's parents lived in the "hill country of Judea" is correct; and then the relationship between Zachariah and the "order" of Abijah—not particularly well-famed[174] —as well as Zachariah's active and actual priestly service in the temple must rest on solid grounds. There is no evidence, furthermore, to question that John's parents were called Zachariah and Elizabeth, even though we do not have any other reliable information about them.[175]

These details, plus the general framework, show that, despite the literary genre employed, the historical and factual dimension goes very deep into the infancy narratives in Mt and Lk. Their authors were moored to solid history and factuality; they were aware that they were dealing with concrete persons who lived and worked in the normal circumstances of a human life at a concrete and well defined period of time, in a particular and perfectly identifiable place. Where theology has not exerted its transfiguring power the bare and harsh factuality of history emerges with all its unimpressiveness and prosaic routine. But this very fact is evidence enough that even where theology sheds a transfiguring light on the reports, we are not to assume that the historical dimension is non-existent—rather the opposite assumption would be correct. The historical event may be there, despite the fact that the dazzling theological light prevents us from catching and sizing up its factuality and proportions.

Inflation of Virgin Births?

It is within this more general framework that the episode of the virginal conception is placed. We may recall here that the external setting of this particular episode is in perfect agree-

---

[174] Strack H.-Billerbeck P., *Kommentar zum NT* II, 68.

[175] Danieli G., 'Storicità di Matteo I-II: Stato presente della discussione,' in *Saint Joseph durant les quinze premiers siècles de l'Eglise,* 58f, thinks that a further criterion to judge about Mt's intention of writing real facts is the presence of OT prophecies to comment on the facts, and the emphasis on Jesus' Davidic descent.

ment with the Jewish law and custom concerning marriage:
a young "virgin" who is betrothed-wedded to a man but who
is not living with him, because she has to be "taken" yet into
her husband's house; a husband who for some reason decides
to dismiss his betrothed wife, has to "divorce" her and Joseph
intends to do so; the situation having been clarified, the husband "takes" his wife to his house. All these details fully
match the legal and customary procedures in a Jewish marriage
at the time. Importantly, both Mt and Lk agree on all this,
except for the contemplation of divorce.

In this marital situation, which both historically and legally
is perfectly identifiable, something happens—the narrative
says—that marks a departure from law, custom and nature:
a) the young betrothed wife conceives a child without man's
intervention; b) it is the divine Spirit that is at work in this
conception. This is the central fact. There are some side
elements, such as apparitions of angels, dreams where God reveals His plan, angelic messages, all of which should not
bother us here. These and other elements are well known to
both the Old Testament and the Jewish religious literature.
They may be regarded as literary devices inherent to the genre
itself, which should not have any more meaning here than
in other extra-biblical narratives of the same nature, where
they are reflections of theological light.

The situation, however, with the central fact of the narrative—virginal conception—is different. Let us say, first of
all, that no one resorts to the pagan legends or hierogamies
any longer to explain the origin and meaning of this central
fact. The entirely semitic character of the narratives in general and of this episode in particular makes it compulsory to
turn to the Jewish literature in order to find the adequate background of the infancy reports.

Now, the Jewish literature, both biblical[176] and extra-biblical,

---

176 Cfr Knoch O., 'Die Botschaft,' 43: "The Old Testament nowhere

does not offer any example where emphasis is laid on the virginity of a mother who conceives a child, and on the Spirit as the only agent in such a conception, the action of any man being positively and explicitly excluded. This realization seems to be beyond any reasonable doubt. The implication is that the detail of a virginal conception in the Gospel narratives cannot be assumed *a priori* to be a literary device or resource of that genre. Such an understanding would have to be proved. We shall see that this is not an easy task.

The biblical literature offers the passage where Is 7:14 refers to the *almah,* girl, who conceives and gives birth to a child. The difficulties to connect this passage with a "virgin" birth are well known—despite the Greek translation of *almah* by *parthenos,* virgin. The extra-biblical literature offers two cases which deserve some attention: the case of Melchizedek in the Slavonic translation of the book of Enoch XXIII, and certain expressions in Philo.

The former certainly reports a virginal conception—by a woman who was not a virgin. Sophonim, Melchizedek's mother, was sterile; she had given no children to Nir, her husband; but when she was old, she conceived without Nir having been with her a long time, and Nir wanted to divorce her. She dies, and when they prepared to bury her, a beautiful child appears beside her body. The boy is hidden for fear of persecution, but in a dream at night Nir is reassured that the child will be saved "and he will be my high priest, Melchizedek forever." Nir blesses the Lord "because your word has created a great priest in the womb of my wife Sophonim." The contacts of this story with the infancy narratives and with the Jewish literature of the same type are obvious, but the contact with Hebr 7 is no less obvious. It is on the basis of

---

speaks about a virgin who through God's miraculous intervention became mother of any of the great men in the history of Israel. The only reference is always to unfruitful women to whom God gives a child in a wondrous way, but it is a child of the seed of her own husband."

these contacts with Hebr 7 that the passage is regarded as a Christian interpolation, the implication being that the reference to a virginal conception does not antedate but rather imitates the Gospel episode. Furthermore, no emphasis is laid on the virginity of Sophonim, who, in fact, had proved to be sterile, and now is old, after a long life with her husband—besides the fact that no mention is made of the divine Spirit, and she has no explanation of the fact: "I do not know how the defilement of my womb was conceived." The narrative is built upon other examples of miraculous births where mothers are either sterile, or old, or conceived without man—thereby showing its secondary character in regard to the only known virginal conception, that of Jesus by Mary. The intentionality of heightening the miraculous aspect by exceptional circumstances (proved sterility, old age, conception without man's seed) together into one case, makes the purely parenetic tendency of the narrative all the more obvious—and the historical dimension all the more suspicious. On the other hand, the Spirit is not mentioned at all; what is more, Sophonim dies—apparently completely unaware of the origin of her maternity, which gives to the narrative a magic flavor. This is not the way God usually acts, even in His miracles; at least the Gospel narratives are radically different in this respect, and this is another trait which renders them more acceptable. All in all, this story remains considerably different from the episode in the infancy narratives. The fragmentary document found in Qumran[177] makes no real difference.

The case of Philo is different. In his work *De Cherubim,* 40–51, Philo continues an allegorical development which starts with the book itself. As different from Adam who "knew" his wife,

[177] Cfr Van der Woude, A. S. 'Melchisedek als himmlische Erlösergestalt in den neugefundenen eschatologischen Midraschim aus Qumran-Höhle,' in *Oudtestamentische Studien,* XIV (Leyden, 1965) 354–473.

Those persons to *whose virtue* the lawgiver has testified, such as
Abraham, Isaac, Jacob and Moses, and others of the same Spirit, are
not represented by him as "knowing" women . . . since we hold
that "women" signifies in figure (*tropikos*) sense-perception . . .
the help-mates of these men are called "women" but are in reality
virtues. Sarah "sovereign and leader," Rebecca "steadfastness in excellence." Leah "rejected and faint" through the unbroken discipline
. . . Zipporah, the mate of Moses, whose name is "bird," speeding
upwards from earth to heaven and contemplating there the nature of
things divine and blessed" (n. 40).

Thus *virtue* receives the divine seed from the Creator, but brings
forth to one of *her own lovers* . . . Again Isaac the all-wise besought God, and through the power of Him who was thus besought,
Steadfastness or Rebecca became pregnant (cfr Gen 25:21). And
without supplication or entreaty did Moses, when he took Zipporah
the winged and soaring *virtue,* find her pregnant through no mortal
agency (cfr Ex 2:22) (ms. 43–47).

God is . . . the father of all things, for he begat them, and the husband of Wisdom, dropping the seed of happiness for the race of
mortals into good virgin soil . . . the union of human beings . . .
turns virgins into women. But when God begins to consort with the
soul, he makes what before was a woman into a virgin again, for He
takes away the degenerate and emasculate passions which unmanned
it and plants instead the native growth of unpolluted virtues (n.
49f).

The text of Philo speaks for itself. It is obvious that it has
nothing to do with the concerns of the Gospel narratives of
the virginal conception. Philo embarks on an allegorizing understanding of the Old Testament in order to demonstrate
his contention that *virtues* are fecundated by God when He
infuses His seed into them. To this effect, availing himself of
the philological meaning of their names, Philo transfigures
the wives of Abraham, etc., into virtues who bear fruit to their

lovers, i.e. virtuous men (husbands). The allegorizing is based on the fact that the Old Testament omits to say that Abraham, Isaac, etc., "knew" their wives, but Philo does not thereby intend to say that Isaac, v. gr., is not a true son of Abraham. As a matter of fact, dealing with the same subject, in *Legum Allegoriae*, III, 218, Philo maintains that "Abraham rejoices and laughs, because he is to beget (*gennan*) Isaac (i.e.), Happiness; and Sarah, who is Virtue, laughs also"—in spite of the fact that immediately afterwards (n. 219) he says that "the Lord begot Isaac; for he is himself Father of the perfect nature, sowing and begetting happiness in men's souls."

Philo's expressions have been submitted to a serious analysis by Grelot.[178] The author stresses that the background of Philo's reasoning is biblical; in fact he refers to Jer 3:4 (whereas, oddly enough, Is 7:14 is not even mentioned). There is nothing of a mythological imagery, let alone factuality, to Philo's allegorical reasoning. Philo does not go beyond a moralizing allegory. Here is Grelot's conclusion:

It is true that, as he interprets the patriarchs' birth allegorically, Philo speaks of germ or seed that God, cause of all generation, sows in the womb of virtues. But his perspective is exclusively that of moral and mystical anthropology, where all images are admitted, provided they convey the doctrine intended exactly: virtues are virgins which conceive thanks to the activity of God, the Creator; and what God sows in them is nothing else but "the Good" (p. 571).[179]

178 Grelot Pierre, 'La naissance d'Isaac et celle de Jésus,' *NRTh* 94 (1972) 562–574.
179 Nellessen E., *Das Kind* 105f, agrees: Philo "intends to say that human virtue is brought into practice through divine power only, and that for this, one has to detach himself from sinfulness. To obtain this he (Philo) avails himself of Old Testament examples which he, however, has to reinterpret in a way unusual even with him. He is aware that he presents an unusual and new doctrine, a secret doctrine . . . Indicative of the difference between the Philonic and Christian understanding of virginity is the statement that Sara 'is ranked once more as a pure virgin.' By this Gen 18, 11 intends to say only that Sara was through with her menses as God's promise came to her."

Solitary Boast

This leaves us with Mary's virginal conception as the first known case in the Jewish world where a woman conceives a man by God's action without man's cooperation. This is something absolutely new which cannot be explained *religions-geschichtlich*. Of course, this is not a positive proof that the fact is historical. But it shows that historicity becomes the only alternative—and this is about all one can expect of historical evidence. It is obvious, in fact, that we have to deal with an old piece of information which goes back to a time very close to the fact reported. The burden of proof that the information is not historically true is on those who refuse to accept the obvious meaning of the document. It is not easy to provide this proof.

In fact, it is obvious that the virginal conception is the very centric subject of a comparatively long literary unit in each of the traditions preserved in Mt and Lk: it is intended *per se* and directly, it is the very object of the narrative, and not a marginal literary element. There is more; it is this fact which is operative in the rest of the narrative: in Mt the reference is always to "the child and his mother," even when Joseph is directly involved as the recipient of a message or as its executioner—there is nothing like "Joseph's child" or "his/your child"; in Lk the situation is the same when the narrative refrains from relating Jesus to Joseph as "his" or "their" child, when Mary gives birth to "her child," and when Mary still is the "betrothed wife" of Joseph as she is about to give birth to the child. The fact that two writers, independently of each other, agree on the same fact and on its importance, is certainly not detrimental to the historical factuality of this event. Pretending that Mt and Lk misunderstood their sources is not a serious proposition; for one thing, this information came to them through different, independent channels, and still they, far away from each other, understood this tradition in the same way, i.e. as an event which happened; for another, it is well known that in their writings the authors of the New Testament do not represent their personal faith only, but they represent the living faith of their communities and, we may safely say, of the Christian community of their times. It is from a living tradition—written or oral—that they received not only a piece of literature but also the meaning this literature had in the understanding of the community as community. If there is any misunderstanding it has to be blamed, not on the writers of the episode we are dealing with, but on the community or communities in which the episode was understood in the particular way it is presented in the written document. Furthermore, the fact that two unrelated persons or communities happen to agree on one and the same point makes it all the more difficult to accept the view that the virgin birth was devised and developed as a theological symbol, i.e. theologoumenon. An agreement of this sort is more easily explained if it is based in factual reality than if it has to be admitted that two unrelated persons or communities happened to understand or interpret one and the same narrative as a pure symbol of a theological concept.

Sometimes the view is expressed that the evangelists were uncritical and credulous individuals who took the dross of popular stories for gold of pure doctrine. This view is contradicted, on the practical level, by the strenuous efforts of the exegetes properly to evaluate the subtle, and often very slight, peculiarities and changes of their writings. We are taught that each one of the evangelists was very selective and careful in choosing, arranging and editing the traditional material. On the documentary level, there are no reasonable grounds to dismiss Luke's contention that the material of his Gospel goes back to the "tradition" or teaching of original "eyewitnesses," and that he, in his turn, "with precision traced the whole sequence of events from the beginning." He refers to the existence of written sources before his Gospel. His statement is not contradicted by the facts. We know that he used Mk and what is usually called the Q source, plus some other source—but we also know that in some episodes he departs from Mk to follow some other information, thereby showing some critical judgment of his own. It is very hard to take Lk's statement for a lie, especially when it is backed by the work itself. Now, Luke's allegation covers, not only the public ministry of Jesus, but also the infancy narratives, which follow right after such an allegation. His personal critical judgment was used in these narratives too. The same thing can be said of Mt.

The mention of the Spirit in connection with the virginal conception also supports the historical dimension of the event. The traditions behind both Mt and Lk, at the same time that they explicitly exclude man's intervention, bring the work of the Spirit into a strong relief in order to provide an adequate explanation of the event they report. The authors of these traditions do not think there is anything magic about such an event. Nor is the power and activity of the Spirit "involved in vain" in the Scriptures in order to explain something (a miraculous deed) which does not even exist. These narratives bring the Spirit into the picture because they understand that the event they describe is as factual and real as is the conception of Isaac, by old and sterile parents beyond the age of fruitfulness, *kata pneuma*—by Spirit (Gal 4:29). The difficulty to be overcome by the power of the Spirit is different in either case (see above 107f), but the factuality of its effectiveness is the same.

Given the semitic and Jewish character of the infancy narratives, another detail in them speaks very eloquently for the factuality of the virginal conception. If Joseph were really the father of the child, it would be extremely difficult to explain how and why a Jewish narrative, permeated by a semitic mentality, pushes the "father" of the child into an obviously secondary background. This applies particularly to the narratives in Mt where Joseph has to assume the role of legal father and protector of the child—still he does not know anything about the origin of the child, admittedly the child is not his, the reference is always to "the child and his mother," but never to the child and his father; the way the literary sequence in the genealogy (1:16) is broken underscores the same reality. But this feature is clear in Lk also, where Mary, the mother, is certainly the second personage on the stage only after Jesus, whereas Joseph remains far back in the dark—far behind Zachariah and even Elizabeth.

As soon as this detail is placed in a semitic perspective, it is obvious nonsense—and an outrageous insult both to the assumed father, mother and child—unless the sources understood themselves to be backed by the facts reported; only on this basis can such a strident departure from all social (and religious) postulates be accounted for. The only other alternative is that the sources try to cover up an illegitimate maternity.

Again, this "down-grading" of a father is a detail which does not derive from the related Jewish literature. It is something new, and against the "philosophy" of that culture. After all, even in other cases of the New Testament the role of the father is predominant. In Gal 4:29 even though Paul stresses that Isaac was born "according to the Spirit," he also stresses that "Abraham had two children . . . one of the free woman" (v. 22), and in Ch. 3 the all-important element is Abraham and "*his* seed"; Abraham's preeminence is again underscored in Rom 4, particularly in vv. 13 and 17–21. Jacob is God's choice, but Isaac's role as his father is clearly and strongly emphasized (Rom 9:10f). In the conception of John the Baptizer the same narrative that denies any significant role to Joseph ascribes to John's father the first place and his part in the birth of John is by no means toned down. But the same thing is true of all other wonderful births found in the Old Testament (Isaac, Jacob, Moses, Samson, Samuel) and in the extra-biblical Jewish literature (Noah, Abraham, Melchizedek,

Isaac, Moses, Samuel, Elijah): the father is always given his adequate place, and he is certainly never denied the honor of being the real father of the child. In the case of Joseph we are at odds with the tradition of the Jewish world.

This long exposition leads to the following verification. At the level of the Gospel the evangelists certainly report the virginal conception of Jesus as a fact which really took place, in the sense the narratives claim. Thereby the evangelists do not report their private and personal conviction, but the conviction of their communities and the conviction of the living tradition behind them. The sources through which this living tradition came to the evangelists understood the event they report, not as a literary device or as a theological disguise, but as a factual reality. Linguistic, historical and cultural considerations show that the origin of this information is a Jewish Palestinian community, and that this goes back at least to some years before 70 A.D.

That the post-biblical Christian tradition understood the virginal conception in factual terms, is proved by the title "Virgin" always attached to the name Mary. If this title does not mean the factual virginity of Mary in the conception of Jesus at least, then it not only does not mean anything, but appears ridiculous. Among all "extraordinary" mothers, only Mary (not Sara, not Rebecca, not Elizabeth, etc.) came to be known as "(the) Virgin." And this since very early times. In various of his epistles[180] Ignatius maintains that Jesus is son of Mary and of God exclusively; and in *Smyrn.* 1 he firmly believes that Jesus was truly born of a virgin.

---

[180] *Eph* 7, 18; *Trall* 9. Admittedly, there were some Christian circles— even in Judaism—in which Christ's virginal conception was denied. But the denial itself is evidence that these same circles knew the belief in the virginal conception. The reason for this statement is that no one stresses the obvious or brings into a special relief what is normal—namely that every human being has a biological father—unless someone else maintains the opposite. The stress on the fact that Jesus had a human father makes sense only if it is a reaction against some other tendency which stressed that he did *not* have a human father.

The most ancient credal formulae of the Christian faith always include the birth of Jesus "from Mary a Virgin" and the Holy Spirit. Not only Joseph's name is foreign to the credal formulae, but also the quality of virginity in Mary is always pointed out, and the Holy Spirit is always mentioned as the explanation of Mary's virginal maternity. These formulae deal, not only and not particularly with Jesus' birth, but with his conception too: the notion of a birth "from Mary" would make sense, but a birth from the Spirit would not. Nor is it difficult to see that the confessional formulations have nothing to do with Gal 4:4; this passage of Paul fails to mention both the virginity of Mary and the activity of the Spirit. It is obvious that such formulations were inspired by the Gospel expressions in Mt 1:18, 20, 23 and Lk 1:27, 35, of which they are but a condensed reproduction.

Indiscretion?

Another question connected with the historicity of the virginal conception is how the evangelists, or the sources before them, came to know about a matter which, by its very nature, is more than confidential. The question is legitimate at a level of concern for research; but as an objection against the virginal conception it does not seem to make much sense. We do not know how the evangelists and other authors of the New Testament came to know the information they hand down in their writings. We do not know, in particular, about the origin of the information peculiar to each one of the evangelists. The same thing applies to all historians of antiquity. Still their information is not rejected just because its origin is not known to us. Factually, however, everybody admits today that the evangelists had sources (oral or written) from which to obtain their information. As pointed out, Luke is very explicit about it right at the beginning of his work: he is diligent in his research, and he refers to eyewitnesses as the origin of the tradition (or of written sources) which he incorporates into his writing. Of course, it is not easy for us to determine the possibilities open to Luke's research, or the effort put into his research—still we do not have any right to assume that he is a professional liar.

In this particular regard two verses in Lk 2 should not be passed over in silence as they often are. In v. 19, in the context of the events in Bethlehem at Jesus' birth, the document says that "Mary was treasuring up (*synterein*) all these things in her heart while pondering (*symballousa*) them." In the context of Jesus' declaration that He is supposed to devote Himself to His Father's interests, and of the family life in Nazareth, v. 51b says that "his mother was treasuring (*diaterein*) all things in her heart." One wonders whether these remarks were made just to characterize Mary as an observing person or to stress her memory or intelligence. Interestingly enough, the same thing is not said of Joseph, nor Zachariah or Elizabeth— but it is said, in the case of John, of others: *"all* who heard all these things stored them up (*tithenai*) in their heart" (1:66). Still there is a difference: in 1:66 those who store the memories are those who hear the commentaries about John, and they ask themselves about the meaning of the child. In the case of Mary, at least in 2:19, there are many others who hear the reports about Jesus (v. 18), but (notice the *de*) only Mary treasures up the memories—and she does not ask herself about the meaning of the child. In both cases, however, one senses that the author of the narrative is pointing to the original sources of the information he is passing on. If this is not the purpose of the remarks—particularly in the case of Mary—one cannot see why the author should insist *twice* on Mary's treasuring up those memories.[181] First of all in 2:51 where no reference is made to "these" definite memories (as in 2:19), but to "all" memories in general. Significantly, from this point (2:51)

---

[181] First of all in 2, 51 where no reference is made to 'these' definite memories (as in 2, 19), but to 'all' memories in general. Significantly, from this point (2, 5) the evangelist enters the common evangelic material known from other sources. The implication is that the things Mary treasured up deal with the narratives up to 2, 51.

the evangelist enters the common evangelic material known to him by other sources. The implication is that the things Mary treasured up deal with the narratives up to 2:51: the memories of Jesus' early days. Any sort of psychological characterization of Mary is beside the point. Importantly, the memories of Mary are not mentioned in the rest of the Gospel material in Luke or elsewhere—they are connected to the infancy narratives exclusively. For good reason: the public ministry of Jesus had other witnesses; His infancy and origins, did not.

When Luke wrote his Gospel and (we may say) when the traditions in the infancy narratives were written, Zachariah and Elizabeth, who were old, as well as John the Baptist and Christ (no information about Joseph) were dead. This can explain why these narratives say that it was Mary (and others, 1:60) who "kept these things in her heart." It is from her and others still alive that these narratives originated.

A close analysis of the two remarks concerning Mary (2:19, 51) is instructive. The form and diction of the remark is basically the same in both places. Now, the expression "all (these) words" in the sense of all (these) things (in both cases) is an obvious semitism; semitic also is the saying (to treasure up or to keep) "in one's heart," in both cases likewise. For the concept of "treasuring or keeping" the passage 2:19 uses *synterein,* whereas 2:51 uses *diaterein;* that they mean the same thing in expressions of this nature is proved by the textual variant in Dan (Theod.) 7:28 where both verbs can translate the Aramaic *nmr* in a sentence like ours ("I kept the word/matter in my heart"), and by the fact that in this particular sentence either one can be used, as we shall see. Significantly enough, however, neither term can be characterized as a "Lukanism" by any means. The former (*synterein*) is never used by Luke or Acts—except here (Lk 2:19); the latter is used only here (2:51) in the entire Gospel, and only once in Acts 15:29 where the meaning is different (to stay away), and these are all the occurrences in the New Testament, whereas the former term is used, besides, in Mt 9:17 and Mk 6:20 only.[182] On the other hand, the entire expression is normal in semitic languages, where various verbs can be used, as the following comparison shows:

Lk	OT
2:19 *he de Maria panta syneterei ta rhemata tauta symballousa en te kardia autes.*	Gen 37:11 *ho de pater dieteresen* (*shmr*) *to rhema.*
2:51 *kai he meter autou dieterei panta ta rhemata en te kardia autes.*	Prov 3:1 *ta de rhemata mou tereito* (*nsr*) *se kardia.*
1:66 *kai ethento pantes . . . (ta rhemata tauta: v. 65) en te kardia auton.*[183]	Dan (Theod.) 7:28 *to rhema en te kardia mou dieteresa/syneteresa* (*nmr*).
	1 Sam 21:13 (12) *kai etheto* (*sim*) *David ta rhemata en te kardia autou.*

This analysis shows that in Lk 2:19.51 there is nothing specifically Lukan, and there is something specifically non-Lukan. The analysis shows, furthermore, that the entire sentence is perfectly semitic in expression and form.[184] The implication is that the remarks concerning Mary (and those in 1:66) go back to the tradition previous to the evangelist, some time before 70 A.D. It is this tradition that points to Mary as "treasuring up" all these memories.

Let us "assume" for a while that the virginal conception of

---

[182] Not even the simple *terein* is a "Lukan" term. It is never used in Lk; in Acts it appears 8 times but with the meaning of keeping/watching a prisoner or a prison, safe in 15, 5 where the reference is to keeping/observing the Law. Lk uses *paraterein* in 6, 7; 14, 1; 20, 20 for watching/spying.

[183] Expressions similar to this one can be found in Lk 21, 14; Acts 5, 4; 19, 21, where the meaning is different though.

[184] The examples from the Old Testament show that the semitic form in Lk 2, 51 has not been altered. A comparison between 2, 19 and 2, 51 shows that in the former case the semitic form has been slightly retouched by the addition of *symballousa*. Luke uses this verb several other times (the meaning is not always the same) both in Lk and in Acts. This, plus the praticipial form, may suggest that this is the only Lukan improvement on the original sentence.

Jesus was real and factual. Who could be the ultimate and final source of such information? Obviously, only Mary—regardless of how close to her and how accurate other sources might have been. Now, it is in this direction that the narratives in Lk point—even though they never say so explicitly. After all, the narratives originated from some Jewish-Christian community in Palestine and go back to some time before 70 A.D., but there is no evidence that they came into being just a few days before that year. Geographically and chronologically the possibility stands that the memories of Jesus' birth and infancy go back to her who "treasured up all these things in her heart." To deny or to ignore this possibility may prove unscholarly and uncritical.

The historical value of the infancy narratives is called into question for theological reasons. It is often contended that the theology, and particularly Christology, with which these narratives operate is very developed and advanced; it belongs to a late period of the Christian faith, when Christ's ontological divine sonship was grasped and believed. The implication being that the infancy narratives are a later creation without concern for historical research and verification, at the service of the Christian faith. Thus, the idea of the virginal conception was devised to support the belief in Jesus' divine sonship. Other questions raised in this connection are: that admittedly Christ was a human being like us "in everything," except sin, but the virginal conception, it is contended, is at variance with this axiom; that Christ could not have been God's Son from the beginning because He showed Himself to be ignorant about many things, and particularly about Himself and about His divinity—the implication being that He could not have been conceived virginally (which implies God's paternity); that the entire episode of the virginal conception is just a *theologoumenon*, i.e., a way to express the great interest and care of God for this man, particularly for His coming into the world. Here follow some reflections on these questions.

Progressive Theology in the Infancy Narratives

From a dialetic point of view, an advanced theology does not exclude historicity. History and theology are two different approaches to one and the same reality. The death of Christ is an historical fact, but its redeeming value is a theological reality. The factuality of Christ's death stands even at the level of the highest and most advanced theological insights into it. Likewise, a developed theology might have placed the virginal conception in a new perspective and bathed it with a new light.

But it does not necessarily mean that theology cannot respect historical facts. We know that it does, as we also know that the theology of the Bible cannot exist without facts since it is from the facts that it draws its teaching. Speculation and theorizing are not the mood of the Bible.

But one wonders whether the Theology-Christology of the infancy narratives is that progressive.

Mt

Let us take Mt. In these narratives Christ is, first of all, "son of David" (1:1; cfr vv. 17.20); but this feature is obviously Jewish-nationalistic, and in all events, it is well established not only in Paul about 55 A.D. (Rom 1:3; 15:12), but also in the primitive Christian preaching preserved in Acts 2:25–31, to which some passages of the Gospel tradition itself, like Mk 12:35–37, should be added. Christ is "son of Abraham" (Mt 1:1; cfr v. 17); but, again, this conviction, with all that it entails, goes back to the Old Testament, is the basis of Paul's theologizing in Gal 3 and 4 (cfr Rom 4) around 55 A.D., and is well attested by the primitive Christian faith in Acts 4:25f. He is "the Messiah" (Mt 1:16f; 2:4); this faith, the most basic and deepest belief of the Twelve, is explicitly stated in archaic formulations of the kerygma like Acts 3:20; 2:36 (cfr 5:42), and goes back, no doubt, to the Gospel records (Mk 8:29; 9:41). To Jesus' Messiahship His birth in Bethlehem is linked (Mt 2:1); the only theological dimension of this detail is its messianic connection, which is based on common Jewish faith built upon Mich 5:1, quoted by Mt 2:5f *in extenso*. In Mt's narrative Jesus is, moreover, "king of the Jews" (2:2); this is certainly not a development of Christian theology, at least not in the sense that Mt mentions this title, which is totally messianic in character according to the Jewish hopes of deliverance and glory—it is a king of the Jews who can frighten Herod, not the king of the Jews enthroned by Pilate (Jn 19: 12–15). Jesus is a "leader" for Mt

2:6, as the Messiah was for Micah; this detail goes back to the Old Testament image of the Messiah, and there is nothing particular about it. Mary's son is precisely Jesus "because he *saves* his people from their sins" (1:21); as early as 1 Thess 1:10 Paul refers to "Jesus the deliverer," as he refers in 5:9 to "salvation through Jesus Christ our Lord" also; the early Christian kerygma in Acts 4:12 maintains that "salvation is not found in anyone else," except Jesus, since there is no other name by which we must be "saved" (cfr v. 9); and the kerygma in Acts 5:11 teaches that God made Him "saviour" (cfr Acts 2:21; 3:15). This latter passage in Acts 5:31 relates Jesus as "saviour" to the "forgiveness of sins" of Israel, which is a concept already present in the preaching of John the Baptizer (Mk 1:4f) and insisted upon in the primitive Christian kerygma in connection with Christ (Acts 2:38; 3:19; 10:43).

A fairly prominent idea in Mt's narratives is the persecution against the newly-born Messiah. The images and the expressions used are important. The Messiah has to go into exile in "Egypt" because "Herod is going to seek the life of the child to suppress him" (Mt 2:13); this is obviously reminiscent of the vicissitudes of Moses as reported in Ex 2:15—as reminiscent of Moses' return from his exile from Madian to Egypt (Ex 4:19) is the angel's order to Joseph to "go to the land of Israel, since those who sought the life of the child are dead" (Mt 2:20). To the perspective of persecution also belongs the slaughter of the holy innocents in Mt 2:16f where the suffering of the Jewish exiles to Babylon is recalled in terms of Jer 31:15. Potential persecution by Archelaus is the reason why Joseph and his family cannot settle in Judah (Mt 2:22f). If this persecution should express the theology of the suffering Messiah—the Servant of the Lord—then it is generally recognized that this conception appears very early in Christian thinking; the reference in 2 Cor 5:21 is unequivocal (cfr Phil 2:7f), but the tradition is much earlier. This sort of theological pattern as it is presented in Is 53 was the scriptural evidence to explain the death of the Messiah to a Jewish audience, and traces of this process can be seen in Acts 3:13 and 8:32ff; it is generally pointed out that the body and blood of Jesus offered "for many" or "for you" is a reference by Jesus Himself to Is 53.

Still, the doctrinal purpose in the narrative of Mt 2 seems well to point in another direction. The connection with Moses' fate has already been noticed. It can be added now that some kind of persecution is the fate of Abraham, Noah and others in the Jewish religious literature of the time—and this persecution always comes from the (pagan) rulers. It seems that the narrative intends to relate and compare Jesus to the most prominent men in Salvation History, to Moses more particularly. The "saviour" of olden times was persecuted by the existing (impious) power—and the saviour of present times touches off the same reaction and undergoes the same exile and suffering by the wordly authority, and is delivered by God by the same means. Thus, the outlook is rather retrospective and completely Jewish: the Messiah is fully rooted in the history of His own people. In this regard, it is noticeable that in the Christian tradition the persecution against the Messiah comes, first of all, from the Jews themselves (1 Thess 2:14; Acts 2:23, 36; 3:13; 4:10f, 25ff, etc.); and this also is the testimony of the Gospel tradition in general. In Mt 2, however, the hostility against Jesus does not come from "his people" but from Herod and Archelaus, who were never regarded as Jews—they are pagan and irreligious rulers, like Nimrod or Pharaoh, in the view of those who wrote these narratives[185] This confirms the meaning of the comparison between Jesus and Moses—and others—expounded above, and suggests that the origin of these narratives is Jewish: the Messiah is welcome

---

[185] Cfr the very archaic passage in Acts 4, 27 where Herod and Pilate are the main persecutors of Christ—though the Christian tradition adds "the people of Israel." Which Herod is this?

among "his people"; it is the foreign rulers who oppose God's deliverance and salvation. This is certainly not a piece of specifically Christian advanced theologizing.

Within such a framework one wonders whether the mention of "his people"—the people of the "saviour"—has a restrictive, nationalistic ring about it in Mt 1:21. At any rate, the "leader" born in Bethlehem rules "my people *Israel*" (2:6; cfr 2:4). To the original community in Jerusalem Peter says that they are the children of the prophets and of the covenant and that it is for them that God sent His Servant (Acts 3:25f).

The reference to the Wise Men who "paid homage" (*proskynein*) (Mt 2:2, 8, 11) means nothing in terms of worship, the inference being that it does not point to Christ's divinity. The same thing applies to the notion of "offering gifts" (Mt 2:11). The Greek verb (*prospherein*) does not necessarily convey the idea of sacrificial offering and recognition of divinity; admittedly the cultic dimension is normal in the use of this term (very often in Lev and Num), but passages like Gen 43: 26; Jud 3:17f; 5:25 (B); 2 Sam 17:29, etc., are evidence that it is not necessarily so. Particularly interesting for Mt 2:11 is Ps 71: 10ff (**LXX**).

The kings of Tarsis and of the isles shall bring gifts (*dora prospherein*); the kings of Sheba and Seba shall offer gifts. Yea, all kings shall pay him homage (*proskynein*); all nations shall serve him.

He will live and will be given the *gold* of Arabia.

These passages, together with Is 60:6; 2 Kings 10:2, 10, form the real background of v. 11 in Mt 2.

The theme of the "star" in Mt 2:1–10 does not make any particular advancement in Christian theology. In point of fact, such a motif is rather unknown to the rest of the New Testament. Whether passages like Mt 4:15f; Eph 4:14; Apc 2:28; 22:16 have anything to do with it is highly questionable at least. Whatever theological elaborations there may be, Mt 2:1–

10 should be related to the messianic[186] oracle of the "star stepping forth out of Jacob" (LXX *anatelei astron*) and with the "sceptre rising out of Israel" in Num 24:17. The theme of the star is known to the Jewish stories about Abraham's birth; and extraordinary light is connected with the stories about Isaac's and Moses' birth.[187] It is to a Jewish traditional background that this concept points.

The Spirit as an agent of God's power (Mt 1:18, 20) for the most various effects is well known to the Old Testament— there is nothing specifically Christian about it. The fact that the power of the Spirit is connected with a virginal conception does not change the character of the theological thought involved. On the other hand, in itself a conception, even a virginal one, by the power of the Spirit, does not imply by necessity a *divine* dimension in the child thus conceived. Paul (Gal 4:29) can say that Isaac was conceived "by power of the Spirit," and yet there is no question of divine dimensions in Isaac. The conception of Jesus through the Spirit does not necessarily involve His divinity—it does not require a highly advanced theologizing about Jesus' divinity, nor is there any evidence that this was the implication seen and intended by the original authors of these narratives.

Nor does the divinity of Christ find stronger support in the name Emmanuel which the author correctly translates as "God with us" (Mt 1:23). If such a name could make good sense to the prophet without deeper implications, the same thing can (and most likely is) true of this author. Nothing suggests that deeper dimensions are operative here.

In Christ's exile into Egypt the oracle of Os 11:1 could be fulfilled: "From Egypt I called *my son*" (Mt 2:15). There is no indication that this language means here much more than it did to the prophet: the concept of election, fatherly tenderness,

186 Cfr Strack H.-Billerbeck P., *Kommentar zum NT* I, 76f.
187 *Ibid.*, 77f.

care, and protection of God; even if in Mt it applies to a single person, and not to the entire people as in the prophet. The deliverer is delivered by God—as Moses was. Messianic overtones could be included: that in New Testament times "son of God" was a messianic title is evidenced by passages like Mk 3:11; 5:7; Jn 1:24—at the level of their "Sitz" in Christ's lifetime—a title which goes back to biblical sayings like 2 Sam 7:14; Ps 2:7; 89:27f, and to early Jewish literature.[188]

God through the prophet Nathan addresses David in these terms: "I will be to him (your son) a father, and he shall be to be a son; if he commit iniquity I will chasten him . . . but my mercy shall not depart from him" (2 Sam).

God addresses the messianic King: "You are my son. This day have I begotten you" (Ps 2).

Again, it is God who speaks to the Messiah: "He shall call unto me: You are my father, my God, and the rock of my salvation. I also will appoint him first-born, the highest of the kings of the earth" (Ps 89).

This only underscores the idea of election, protection, etc. Obviously, deeper contents can be read into the expression, but they must come from outside the narratives, not from the text itself nor from the Jewish atmosphere where it belongs.

The only other Christological dimension in Mt's narratives is that Jesus is *Nazoraios* (2:23). The document links this title to the town of Nazareth. If there is but a geographical connotation to *Nazoraios,* no theological question arises. If there are deeper theological implications it has to be noticed that no theology has been built by the New Testament on this title, and that, as a matter of fact, the author of Mt 2:23 refers to "prophetic" theology, i.e. to the Old Testament—no matter whether the meaning of the title is (the Davidic) "twig"

---

[188] Strack H.-Billerbeck P., *op.c.* III, 15–20, 675ff.

(*nezer* in Hebrew, cfr Is 11:1) or "saved" (*nazur*, cfr Is 49:6; Ez 6:12) or *nazir*, i.e. consecrated to the Lord (cfr Num 6:5– 8).

This survey covers all the Christological concepts in Mt's narratives. The theological ideas involved are not those of a developed Christian thought—indeed they are perfectly Jewish and do not go beyond the theology of the Old Testament. The new element of a virginal conception itself does not fall beyond this framework, since in this narrative it is presented just as a miracle of God's power—not as the evidence or basis of any divine dimension in the child. There is nothing of a "three stage" Christology here. Indeed, there is but a "one stage" Christology.

In fact, for our purpose what is missing is as important as what is there. In the first place one misses any mention or indication of a pre-existence of Christ—an idea explicitly stated by Paul (2 Cor 8:4; 1 Cor 10:4; Rom 1:3; then, Phil 2:6) as early as 55 or 56 A.D. The notions used by the Gospel narrative for Christ's coming into existence are the normal terms to be begotten, to be born[189] (*gennan* 1:20; 2:4; *tiktein* 2:2; cfr 1:21) which, in the absence of any hint of pre-existence, do not mean the same thing as "becoming flesh" (Jn 1:14) or "becoming a slave" (Phil 2:7). Furthermore, in Mt 1:18 Christ's coming into existence is described as a *genesis* (the best attested reading), which, were its proper meaning to be pressed, would imply ignorance of any concept of pre-existence (cfr Jn 8:58 Abraham *ginetai;* Christ *esti*). Obviously, the first stage of any "three stage" Christology is missing.

But, then, any idea of an everlasting life of Christ, any idea of resurrection and heavenly glorification of the Messiah is completely foreign to Mt's narrative also. Foreign to them is any concept of (Christian) eschatology, parousia, judgment,

---

[189] Normally, likewise, the mother "is with child" (1, 18.23) and "gives birth" (1, 21–23).

theology of the Son of Man etc., too. The implication is that the third stage of any "three stage" Christology is not represented at all. Incidentally, none of the major themes or problems of the Gospel tradition, or of the Christian doctrinal development, or of the life of the community, can be found in these narratives—not even the title *kyrios*. All we find is "king" of the Jews (2:2).

Lk

The setting to evaluate the Christology in Lk's narratives is provided by two statements that say the same thing. One is in 2:40: "the child (Jesus) was growing up and was gaining strength, filled with wisdom, and the grace of God was upon him." The other is in 2:52: "Jesus was progressing steadily in wisdom and age (or size) and grace before God and men." Obviously, these statements do not represent a highly developed theology. If anything, they are rather at variance with it. On the other hand, almost the same statements are made about John the Baptizer (Lk 1:80a, 66) and of Samuel (1 Sam 2:21, 26):

The child Samuel grew before the Lord . . . The child Samuel grew on, and increased in favor both with the Lord, and also with men.

Perhaps the central passage for the present discussion is the Annunciation itself. Mary's son is described as follows: his name will be Jesus, "he will be great and will be called son of the Most High; the Lord God will give him the throne of his father David; he will be king of the house of Jacob forever, and his kingdom will have no end" (Lk 1:32f). It is obvious that this description does not go beyond the doctrine of the Old Testament. It is a perfectly Jewish expression of messianic contents. Greatness can be ascribed even to John the Baptizer (Lk 1:15), but for messianic overtones see 2 Sam 7:9 and Ps 89:28:

God speaks to David through Nathan: "I will make you a great name like unto the name of the great ones that are on earth" (2 Sam).

I will appoint him first-born, the highest of the kings of the earth (Ps 89).

The succession to David's throne obviously goes back to 2 Sam 7:12–16 and Ps 89:20–38 (cfr also Ps 72:5, 17).

When your (David's) days are fulfilled . . . I (God) will set up your seed after you . . . and I will establish your kingdom . . . I will establish the throne of his kingdom for ever . . . And your house and your kingdom shall be made sure for ever before you; your throne shall be established for ever (2 Sam)

I (God) have exalted one chosen out of the people. I have found David my servant. I anointed him; with whom My hand shall be established. My arm also shall strengthen him . . . For ever will I keep for him my mercy, and my covenant shall stand fast with him. His seed also will I make to endure for ever, and his throne as the days of heaven . . . His seed shall endure for ever, and his throne as the sun before me. It shall be established for ever as the moon; and be steadfast as the witness in the sky (Ps 89).

A kingdom over "Jacob" is referred to in Ps 78:81; the notion of "house of Jacob" is found in Is 2:5; 7:17; 10:20; 14:1; 29:22, etc. That the Messiah was to be "son of David" (cfr "David his father"; see 1:69 also) is, admittedly, Old Testament and Jewish doctrine. In this anthology of messianic references it is obvious that "being called son of the Most High" is a dimension of the Messiah which goes back to 2 Sam 7:14 ("I will be a father for him, he will be a father for me"), Ps 2:7 ("you are my son") and Ps 89: 27f[190] ("he shall call unto me: You are my father . . . I also will appoint him first born") as pointed out above (188). This last remark applies to Lk 1:35 where

---

[190] Cfr George A., 'Jésus Fils de Dieu dan l'évangile selon Saint Luc,' *RB* 72 (1965) 190; Benoit P., 'L'Annonciation,' 202.

the child to be born of Mary will be called "son of God"; in such a messianic context, this name is sufficiently explained by an Old Testament background. True, it is possible, and in my view highly likely,[191] that Luke read much more than a messianic title into this name at the time he wrote his Gospel. But, then, a distinction has to be made between the different levels or *Sitze*, of tradition.[192] The original level of this tradition had an Old Testament orientation. The same remarks are valid for Lk 2:49 where Jesus declares that He had to concern Himself with the interests of "my father."

Within the context of the conception, through the Spirit, of the Messiah "son of God," the Messiah is said to be something "holy" (*hagios*). Obviously, the holiness of the Messiah, at this level, does not imply a divine dimension—whatever the relationship to be preferred. In Lk 2:23 Jesus is implicitly said to be holy in the sense of "sacred" (to God) because He is a firstborn son, according to Ex 13:2 (*qaddesh*); in the same way, a "Nazir" is "sacred" (*qadosh*) to the Lord (Num 6:5–8), where the concept of consecration is predominant:

All the days of his vow of Naziriteship there shall no razor come upon his head; until the days be fulfilled in which he consecrates (*nzr*) himself to the Lord, he shall be *holy* (*qadosh*) . . . All the days of his Naziriteship he is *holy* (*qadosh*) unto the Lord.

Furthermore, God had "sanctified" (*hiqdish*) or consecrated Jeremiah as a prophet before he had come forth out of the womb (Jer 1:5; cfr Gal 1:15). It is likely that the word in Lk 1:35 has various harmonics, but the predominant one is, no doubt, that of "consecration," or putting aside, of something chosen and elected. The Gospel tradition records the messianic

---

[191] All the more so if v. 35 is a creation of Luke, as Legrand L., *'L'Arrière-plan néo-testamentaire de Lc, I, 35,'* 70 (1973) 161–192 contends.
[192] Cfr Benoit P., *op. c.* 212ff.

title "holy one of God" applied to Jesus (Mk 1:24; Jn 6:69).
On the other hand, no significant Christian theology was built
in the New Testament on Christ's "holiness." At any rate, in
Lk 1:35 there is no reason why the holiness of the Messiah
should indicate any degree of divine holiness or transcendence.[193]

As for the virginal conception through the Spirit the considerations on Mt are valid here too. The concept of "redemption" in 1:68; 2:38 has nothing to do with the same concept
in the Christian theology proper, but it is the Old Testament
idea of deliverance,[194] which is the same thing as "salvation"
(1:69), even where (1:77) salvation means forgiveness of
sins—particularly when it is God who brings help to Israel
(1:54, 73). This provides the setting for the notion "saviour"
in 2:11, 30, which is nothing but a translation-application of
the name "Jesus"; this is particularly clear in 2:30 on account
of its Hebrew background in Is 52:10. This saviour is understood in terms of the consolation of Israel expected by Symeon
(2:25), of the "redemption of Jerusalem" expected by many
(2:38), and of the "deliverance from our enemies" (1:71) in
order to be set "free from their hands" (1:74) that Zachariah
sees already realized. There is nothing specifically Christian
about these ideas. The Messiah, after all, remains the glory
of God's "people Israel" (2:32, 34). And this is the "people"
to which John the Baptizer announces salvation through redemption of sins (1:77). In this perspective the saviour is
born precisely "for you" (2:11); is not Israel the "men whom
God loves" (2:14)? There seems to be a restricted (or more
central) notion of "people" in these narratives: the Messiah
is (in the first place at least) for Israel (cfr Acts 3:25f).
Even if, in agreement with Is 42:6; 49:6, the Messiah also is

---

[193] Even Schneider G., 'Jesu geistgewirkte Empfägnis,' 115, agrees that
there is nothing here of a "Wesenschristologie" proper that implies a physical
divine sonship. He suggests ("vielleicht") the concept of "new creation"
starting with Christ—which plays no role in Luke's theology.
[194] Büchsel, *ThWNT* IV, 353f.

"light of the gentiles" (Lk 2:3f), this kind of universalism does not mark any theological progress beyond Isaiah.[195]

Obviously, there is nothing specifically Christian, either, in the idea of light, rise or splendor (1:79; 2:9, 32) accompanying the coming of the Messiah. In Lk 2:34 Symeon foresees that the present Messiah will be the downfall and the rise of many "in Israel," a sign that will be opposed. This was clear to everyone who witnessed the development of Christ's relations and break with the Jews of His time in Palestine. About 55 A.D. Paul elaborates on this theme to a certain length (Rom 9–10), but he can provide Old Testament evidence for this (9:24–33), particularly the text of Is 8:14; 28:16:

The Lord shall be for a sanctuary; but also for a stone of stumbling and for a rock of offence to both the houses of Israel, for a gin and for a snare to the inhabitants of Jerusalem. And many among them shall stumble, and fall, and be broken, and be snared, and be taken.

Behold, I (God) lay in Sion for a foundation a stone, a tried stone, a costly cornerstone of sure foundation; he that believes shall not make haste.

The same point, however, is pressed in the very early Christian preaching (Acts 4:10f, etc.), and goes back to the synoptic tradition (Mk 12:1–12, etc.). This detail does not necessitate a high development in Christian theology.

Occasionally Jesus is referred to as "Christ" (2:11, 26). Obviously, in the expression "the Christ of the Lord" (2:26) the functional dimension of the name is obvious, it means but the Messiah (the Anointed); it is not a proper name. The case in 2:11 appears more complicated: a savior was born "who is *christos kyrios*" (Christ Lord). The first complication is of

[195] Schürmann H., 'Aufbau,' 110, stresses that the passage of the Annunciation (Lc 1, 26–36) in the words of the angel in 1:30–33 contains an "uralten Kern und judenchristliche Christologie." The totality almost of ch. 2 (vv. 1–39) reflects, in Schürmann's view, a Palestinian origin.

a textual order, since the two Greek words transcribed offer many variations in the textual tradition. It is not unlikely that the textual changes are just witnesses to some uneasiness to understand what seems to be the authentic reading—the one we have transcribed. The meaning of the supposedly authentic reading is not easy to see;[196] it is difficult to explain even grammatically. Syntactically, the entire sentence is an incidental expression which might very well be an insertion into a pre-existing narrative. "Formally," the saying is reminiscent of Acts 2:36, even though the difference should not be overlooked. Grundmann's[197] view is that by such a formulation Luke "creates the link between the Jewish Christian confession of Jesus as the Messiah, and the confession of the gentile community in Jesus the Lord." If so, this would be one of the "Lukan" retouches at the "redactional" level—but nothing else. To this question the passage of Lk 1:43 is related, where Elizabeth speaks about "the mother of my Lord." Nothing in the text suggests the idea of divinity in any way. On the other hand, this could be another retouch by Luke. This, however, is not easy to admit. Sometimes the authors of the New Testament, Luke included (Acts 1:14), refer to the "mother of Jesus," but never is Mary called the mother of the Lord. Furthermore, it is well known that in the Old Testament kings—and persons of authority or dignity—are referred to as "my lord" (1 Kings 1:13–47). Passages like Mk 12:36f show that the expression "my lord" in Ps 110:1 ("Yahweh said to my Lord") applied to the Messiah in the Jewish understanding of the Psalm[198]—and this continues in the early Christian tradition (Acts 2:34–36; 8:56; 1 Cor 15:25). If it was believed that David called the Messianic king "my lord," everybody else in the Jewish community could adopt this usage. The mention of the mother is accidental.

That the "Spirit" goes from Mary or from her child to

---

[196] Cfr Grundmann, *ThWNT* IX, 525 and fnt 276.
[197] *Ibid.*
[198] Cfr Strack H.-Billerbeck P., *Kommentar zum NT* IV, 458ff.

others (Lk 1:41; cfr 1:15)—if this is the case—is not to be related to any sort of premature "Pentecost." The Old Testament offers examples which can be compared with this: the Spirit which was on Moses is shared with 70 other people (Num 11:17, 24f); with the mantle of Elijah, Elisha inherits the prophetic Spirit of his master in a double measure (2 Kings 2:9–15; cfr 1 Sam 10:10ff; 19:20–24).

The "intelligence" of Jesus at twelve is strongly stressed in Lk 2:47. It is clear, however, that we are worlds apart from the idea of a divine wisdom or knowledge in Christ. The tendency of the text certainly is to present an extraordinary child with extraordinary gifts. This tendency is well represented in the Jewish religious literature concerning Abraham[199] and Moses;[200] an echo of the tradition concerning Moses can be heard in Acts 7:20–22.

Finally, a detail which regards John the Baptizer. In Lk 1:17, 76 John is clearly portrayed as the forerunner of the "Lord" and is interpreted as being the Elijah who was to come in order to prepare the people for the day of Jahweh. No doubt we have a piece of Christian reflection on the roles both of John and of Jesus. This cannot be interpreted in the light of the Old Testament or of the Jewish religious literature. It is an obvious case where Christian theology crept into an otherwise Jewish (Christian) tradition. Still, it is to be noticed that this theological reflection does not necessitate the highest development in the Christology of the New Testament. As a matter of fact, such an understanding of John is already found in the earliest stages of the synoptic tradition and in the most archaic sections of the fourth Gospel (in Ch. 1 and 3 with an echo in 5:33–36; 10:40f), with some reminiscences in Acts (1:5, 22; 10:37; 11:1, 6; 13:24; 19:4). Paul does not show the slightest concern about this question.

On the other hand, we miss in Luke's narratives the same

[199] Jubilees II, 14–24.
[200] Flavius J., *AJ* 11 IX, 6, etc.

items of a Christian developed theology that we miss in Mt. There is no reference at all to any sort of pre-existence of Jesus. On the contrary, the expressions used in this connection are those which apply to every child: conception (1:31; 2:21); generation (1:35), child-birth (1:31; 2:7, 11), fruit of the womb (1:42), firstborn (of the mother, 2:7), male child opening the womb of his mother (2:23). Not even the slightest reference is made to Jesus' resurrection and endless life, to His parousia, etc. These narratives know nothing of a "three stage" Christology.

Summing Up

This analysis of the infancy narratives both in Mt and in Lk shows that their theological ideas represent a very primitive Christology. What is more, this analysis shows that there is almost nothing specifically Christian to these narratives. The various concepts by which the person and role of the Messiah are portrayed are those of the theology of the Old Testament or of the Jewish extra-biblical literature of the time. Instead of Christology in these narratives, one might speak of something like "Messianology."

The main implication of this conclusion is that the idea of a virginal conception for Christ has nothing to do with the highest developments of Christology in the New Testament. In other words, the virginal conception is not a theological necessity or convenience created by the realization of Christ's pre-existence, divinity, and divine sonship—which, supposedly, was considered incompatible with a human paternity. Such developments and such concerns are completely foreign to the narratives in general, and to the "annunciations" in particular, where the concerns are merely "messianic," and not Christological or theological.

The rather primitive theological framework in which the doctrine of Jesus' virgin birth is set in Mt and Lk is in sharp contrast with another fact. If the conceptualization and the narratives of the virgin birth is a theologoumenon necessitated, or at least prompted, by a highly developed Christion theology that came to grasp that Christ was God, how is it that in the great New Testament theologians this kind of theologoumenon plays no role at all? Why should it be so prominent *only* in narratives so deeply semitic and so primitive in Christian thinking? It is obvious, in fact, that neither in Paul nor in John, Peter or Hebrews does the doctrine of the virgin birth play any significant role; it is so much so that, as pointed out above, the silence of the New Testament except for Mt and Lk, is brought up as evidence against the existence of such a belief in early Christianity. Both the author of Hebrews, John and Paul are very emphatic on Christ's divine dimension and on his particular relationship to God. Still they never build any kind of evidence on such a belief, nor do they mention it in connection with their affirmations concerning Christ's "equality" with God. There is no evidence that they ever thought in terms of such a theologoumenon, and still less that they fabricated it.

A confrontation of this attitude of the New Testament theologians with that of Ignatius of Antioch is really instructive. In fact, Ignatius knows that the faithful of Smyrna are "thoroughly convinced, in regard to our Lord, that he is in truth of the race of David according to the flesh, God's Son by the will and power of God, that he has truly been born of a virgin (*parthenos*)" (*Smyrn.* 1 1). In his epistle to the *Eph.* 7 1 he writes that Christ comes "not only of Mary but also (*kai . . . kai:* see Liddle-Scott A V) of God"; and *ibid.* 18 2 Ignatius maintains that "One God Jesus Christ was conceived by Mary by the dispensation of God of the seed of David but (*de*) of the Holy Spirit"; immediately afterwards, 19 1, he adds that "the virginity of Mary, her child-bearing and the death of the Lord were hidden from the prince of this world: three mysteries of proclamation (to be proclaimed) which were accomplished in the stillness of God." As he warns the Trallians against some doctrinal errors (c. 6–8), Ignatius requests them "to be deaf

The Virgin Birth

when anyone speaks to you apart from Jesus Christ who was of the race of David, who was of (*ek*) Mary . . . who also was truly raised from the dead when *His* Father raised him up, as *His* Father shall raise us up . . ." (*Trall.* 9 1f).

Shortly after the Johannine literature was produced, Ignatius insists on the belief on Mary's virginal conception. Still Ignatius is not a theologian but a pastor. He does not theologize at all; he just enunciates the tenets of the Christian faith. It is so much so that, with the only exception of *Eph.* 7 1, the statement on Jesus' virgin birth is always found in the context of credal formulae, very much like our credo, where the main "mysteries" of Christ are spelled out. Neither did Ignatius understand his belief on the virgin birth as a theologoumenon nor did he use it as such theologoumenon to the effect of drawing any conclusions from it. Still he is certainly a witness to the faith of Jesus' virginal conception.

Ignatius' statements teach something more too. The pastoral tone of his words clearly shows that he is not teaching anything new to the communities of Asia Minor. The doctrine of the virgin birth was part of the Christian faith professed by these communities—which becomes all the more apparent when Ignatius warns them against heretics and wants them to "refrain from strange food, which is heresy" (*Trall.* 6 1) and to "be deaf therefore when anyone speaks to you apart from Jesus Christ" (*ibid.* 9 1). The implication is that such a faith was known and held in those communities shortly after the Johannine literature was written; and there is no indication that such faith was accepted there just the day before Ignatius arrived. These communities, furthermore, are Johannine and Pauline communities: Ephesus (cfr Apc 2:2), Smyrna (Apc 2:8); Tralles is close to Ephesus, at any rate much closer than Laodicaea (Apc 3:14; cfr Col 4:15). On the other hand Ignatius certainly represents the faith of the community of Antioch. One wonders whether the author of the Johannine literature—who wrote much later than both Mt and Lk and who was familiar with the entire area of the Ignatian letters (particularly Ephesus —could be ignorant of the belief on the virgin birth. And then his silence and his high theology would be of little support to the view that the virgin birth is a theologoumenon at the service of a developed process of theologizing.

Another important implication is this. This conceptional analysis confirms the results of an historical analysis, namely: the infancy narratives derive from a Jewish milieu, and they go back to a rather early time. The theological evidence refers the reader to a time when the followers of Jesus still thought in Old Testament terms and conceptualized in "pre-Christian" categories. What is Christian about them is that "this" particular child is the Messiah of the Jewish hopes and expectations—but that is about all. The theological developments of the Pauline thought are conspicuously absent from these narratives.[201] This takes us to a time considerably earlier than 70 A.D., even though it would be but a wild guess to put a date on these narratives. The narratives in Mt look more archaic—or at least more Jewish.

[201] Schürmann H., 'Aufbau,' 111, refers to a time from "10 to 20" years earlier—which could be a conservative estimate. Danieli G., 'A proposito delle origini,' 317, is of the view that "we should go back some twenty years at least" beyond the composition of Mt and Lk.

A) Christ is a man like everybody else—except sin. This remains an axiom of every Christological endeavor. But it is not easy to see how Christ's true humanity interferes with a virginal conception. Being human does not imply any necessary relationship with the way one becomes man. Admittedly, the normal course of nature is that a human being is the fruit of two parents, conceived and developed in the mother's womb, matured and "born" after nine months. This, however, is a fact of nature—it is not a metaphysical necessity. A child born by Caesarean section is not born like everybody else, but no one has ever said that he is less human. Premature or even abortive children who can be helped to a normal life are not like everybody else in this respect, but they are not less human. Fecundation by artificial insemination does not render the child not-human. Science will soon offer us "laboratory babies"; I wonder if anyone will say they are not human. Of course, these cases are not the same thing as a virgin birth; still they show different cases in which the way one comes to exist does not interfere with one's being human. But another possibility opens up: suppose that science reaches the point of developing life itself and, then, develops a being with all the characteristics and qualities of a human creature. Would this being be a man— or what? Those who propound polygenism have never contended that only one or the other of the hypothetical groups was or is human, with the exclusion of the others.

The narratives of the Gospel do not pretend that in the case of Christ they are dealing with the normal fact of nature; they rather make it abundantly clear that they understand the virginal conception to go beyond the fact of nature—they ascribe it to the Spirit and *power* of God. In this as in other matters, to deny the virginal conception on grounds that Christ had to be truly human could indicate a "failure to understand the Scriptures and the power of God" (Mk 12:24). Suppose that God in His power decides to bring into being one or several human creatures identical to any other human persons —except for the fact that no parents are involved. There is no reason, on this assumption, to maintain that their "humanity" is different from others' or that they are not as human as everybody else. They would not have a biological connection with the present human family, but this is a different question. Think of polygenism. In Christ, however, His connections with this humanity we know are established through Mary, a daughter of "this" human family.

It is not clear, on the other hand, what "being perfectly human" means in such an objection. No one would maintain that Christ was not perfectly human because He was not a female, or male and female at the same time—both male or female are perfectly human, and yet one is not the other. What I suggest is that the definition of "human" in such a context is not an easy one, or, at least, no such definition has been provided. But the example given proves that someone's connection with the human family through a woman only is sufficient to make this person a member of the entire family, since a woman is perfectly human also.

Being human can mean not to be less than a human being, v.gr. not to be an animal. But, then, animals also supposedly are perfect animals if they are the fruit of two parents. The result is that being the child of two parents is nothing specifically human. Even at the level of the fact of nature, being human depends on one's origin from "human" elements, from human sources—Mary was such a source, and what she provided for the generation of Jesus were truly human elements.

In the present objection the use of the principle that Jesus was like us in everything but sin is certainly abusive—and does not render the meaning of Hebr 4:15. Being mentally deranged is human because it happens to human beings, but being mentally balanced is human too; being mentally retarded is human, but being smart (and even a genius) is human too; and the same thing can be said of human perversions like homosexuality, etc. What is suggested is this: that someone being human does not mean that he has to display in himself the sum total of all human limitations, shortcomings, handicaps, etc. On the assumption that such an individual should ever exist, I do not think that he should be regarded as more fully human than somebody else, or that he is the archetype of humanity. I do not think that only the basest and lowliest human condition is truly human. The implication is that dignity, nobility and even supernatural glory are compatible with true humanity.

Being truly human, therefore, does not exclude being, having, something that not every human being is or has. Plato, Leibnitz, Einstein were no less human because they were geniuses; still they had something more or better than others have. Suppose that in Jesus there was some other dimension higher than humanity. This would not imply that He was not truly human; it would merely imply that he was human—plus something else. If this something else were the cause why Jesus would have to be born of a virgin, it would not exclude that He were perfectly human.[202]

Obviously, the discussion has led us to the relationship between Christ's divinity and his virginal conception. As a matter of fact, both ideas are independent and do not of necessity, go together. Still it is often maintained that the idea of the divinity of Christ necessitates his virginal conception (He has

---

[202] Cfr the valuable considerations offered by Galot Jean, 'La Conception virginale du Christ,' *Greg* 49 (1968) 663ff, particularly this: "In the Immanuel it is not enough to keep the 'with us' only: he who is with us is God and must reveal himself as such. Jesus cannot restrict himself to his being humanly close to men; he must render God the closest possible to them. Had he come in the way of a man like others, without any difference, he would not have revealed himself as 'God with us' in his coming" (663). "By pretending that Jesus would have been less human because of Mary's virginity, one is bound to admitting that he would have been less human because of the celibate life he chose to lead on earth" (665).

to be Son of God), and then He is not truly human; and so the virginal conception is either to be denied together with Christ's divinity and thus He becomes truly human, or is a symbolic device (theologoumenon) to express the peculiarity (divinity) of Christ. Whereas the question of the theologoumenon will be taken up shortly, the foregoing considerations were anticipated to show that true humanity in Christ does not exclude being more than just human, even in the case that Jesus' divine nature necessitated a virginal conception—a necessity, however, that in my view is not real. At any rate, the New Testament grounds the virginal conception, not on a metaphysical necessity, but on the *factual* intervention of God's power —whatever one may think about the methaphysical reasons that theological speculation can provide.[203]

B) The virginal conception is a theologoumenon. It is often said that the episodes in Mt and Lk which indicate a virginal conception do not intend to mean that a virginal conception actually took place, i.e. that Jesus was conceived without a human father. What these episodes intend to portray, it is contended, is the importance of Jesus and His theological significance in God's design: an important man in whom God was highly interested, and for whom God cared in a very particular way. The episode of the virginal conception becomes a theological symbol. This is what a theologoumenon is—regardless of nuances and various possible emphases.

Now, the Jewish tradition, both biblical and extra-biblical, knows several cases of miraculous births: Abraham, Isaac, Moses, Samson, Samuel, etc. In the New Testament Luke, besides the conception of Jesus, reports the miraculous conception of John the Baptizer. Why should the miraculous conception only of Jesus be a theologoumenon? All these men were very important in God's plan of salvation, and He had a particular providence for them. Of course, it can be said that we have to do with theologoumena in all these cases—though this would be difficult to accept (if historical reality is excluded altogether) in the cases of Isaac, Samuel and even John the Baptizer.

Still, even if one admits all these cases to be as many theologoumena, the question remains as to why the theologoumena should have different representations. The traditional cliché to express this sort of theologoumenon was sterility, either by nature's failure or by age. This cliché was still good for John's conception in Lk's narratives. Why should this cliché not convey the same basic idea in the case of Christ? The recourse to a virginal conception marks a break with the literary and "theological" tradition, and brings into the picture something to which the religious language and the religious mentality in which its sprung was not used, not prepared to accept or to interpret correctly—in fact, the interpretation given to it was "historical" and factual, not that of a theologoumenon. At any rate, it was not the obvious "symbol" at hand. Why this difference, why this change, why this innovation, why this "unusual" symbol? The theologoumenon theory has yet to answer this question convincingly.[204] Of course, the situation does not change when the word "Christologoumenon" is preferred.

The "roots of the Christologoumenon" are summarized by Schneider.[205] In the first place one resorts to Ps 2, 7, where God addresses his Messiah with the words "you are my son, today I have begotten you." The Qumran literature is mentioned in this connection too; in 1QSa 2, 11f the author, thinking of Ps 2, 7, refers to the time "when God will beget the Messiah among them." The passage of Is 7, 14 (the *almah* will conceive etc.) was operative in the process towards Jesus'

---

[204] All these considerations apply to an understanding of Mary's virginity as expressing the theological concept that she "belongs to God alone," that she "lives and conceives only from God": cfr Steinmetz Franz-Joseph, 'Geboren aus Maria der Jungfrau,' *Geist und Leben* 43 (1970) 460.

[205] Schneider G., 'Jesu geistgewirkte Empfängnis,' 113f.

"virginal" conception, in the sense that its translation by *parthenos* in Greek "could" be understood of a virgin proper. Since Jesus had to be something more than John the Baptizer, He was made to be born of a "virgin" and to owe His own existence to the Spirit—and not just to be filled with the Spirit even before His birth. Through such an understanding of Is 7, 14 the early Christians established a link with the legends of the gentiles, which would become a means to draw them to Christ.

But the same author admits that all this is *"sehr hypothetisch."* It is all the more so, since this is a second step, after his first step attempting to establish that there was a pre-synoptic story about Jesus' "spirit-affected" conception without the concept of virginity—a tradition which, he has to grant, "cannot be recovered with certainty." Furthermore, the same author has to avow that the pre-synoptic tradition of a conception affected by the Spirit cannot be established in Palestinian Judaism, Qumran religiosity included.[206] To this it may be added that Ps 2, 7 makes no reference to a generation through the Spirit, or of a "virgin"; what is more, there is no evidence that Ps 2, 7 plays any relevant role in these narratives (which it does in the baptism narrative, Mk 1, 11 paral., or in Acts 13, 33, etc). Schneider[207] himself raises the question as to how (and why) Jesus' conception and birth was linked to the activity of the Spirit. In his view, the answer may (*"wohl"*) have to come from the baptism revelation where Ps 2, 7 is related to Jesus' fullness of the Spirit. The problem is, however, that, otherwise than in baptism, this Ps is not mentioned in Lk 1, 31ff, nor is there in Lk 1 any particular mention of Christ being filled with the Spirit.

The historical origins of the theologoumenon-theory go back

---

[206] Nellessen E., *Das Kind,* 103: all this can mean "that the Messiah is born by God's intervention, but not otherwise than all men are, and that the divine generation takes place at the entrance upon the messianic office."

[207] Schneider G., *op. c.*

to *"religionsgeschichtliche"* considerations.[208] As pagan myths
proved unsuccessful to explain the virgin birth in the Gospels,
hellenistic Judaism was brought into the picture as the historical and doctrinal antecedent of the Gospel narrative. This
was the choice of Dibelius, followed by Guthknecht and
Malet.[209] The grounds for a Judeo-hellenistic theologoumenon
of a conception by God's intervention are found in Paul's statement that Isaac was "born according to the Spirit" (Gal 4, 29),
and the text of Philo, quoted above, where he refers to biblical
women as symbols of virtues activated by God. Such an idea
in hellenistic Judaism does not derive from the Bible, it is
contended, but rather from a belief in Egypt according to the
testimony of Plutarch[210] (c. 46–120) in New Testament times:

And yet the Egyptians make a distinction here which is thought
plausible, namely, that while a divine spirit can approach a woman
and produce some germs of being [in her] there is no such thing
as carnal intercourse and communion between a man and a divinity.

The application of this line of thought to the virgin birth
of the Gospels has been proved groundless by Grelot and
Nellessen.[211] It is emphasized that the idea of a virgin birth
through divine generation is completely foreign to the pre-
Christian Jewish tradition. More and more strongly voiced,
furthermore, is the idea that the History of Religion cannot
offer authentic parallels to the evangelic understanding of the
virgin birth. Nellessen[212] maintains "that a parallel that could

---

[208] Cfr Danieli G., 'A proposito delle origini,' 319ff.

[209] Dibelius M., 'Jungfrauensohn und Krippenkind . . .,' in *Botschaft
richte der Heidelberger Akademie . . .*, 4 1932); Guthnecht G., *Das und
Geschichte* I (Tübingen, 1953) 1–78 (first published in *Sitzungsbe-Motiv der
Jungfrauengeburt in religions—geschichtlicher Beleuchtung* (Greifswald,
1952); Malet A., *Les évangiles de Nöel: Mythe ou réalité?*, (Alethina 1),
(Paris, 1970).

[210] *Vita Numae* 4, 4.

[211] Grelot P., 'La naissance d'Isaac,' 472–487; 561–574; Nellessen E., *Das
Kind*, 103ff.

[212] Nellessen E., *op. c.* 108. In the same direction, Vawter B., *This Man*

provide a model for the whole contents of the formulation of the Christian faith is not known so far."

On the other hand, the contribution of Philo's speculation to this doctrine has already been discussed. He engages in an allegorizing exposition of the scriptural text designed to fit the needs of his intent. In doing so, he is very personal, and the entire allegorizing process is his own work. He does not betray any influence of the Egyptian belief reported by Plutarch upon his thought. In the first place, in Plutarch's text the concept of virginity is not even mentioned; however the activity of the spirit was thought of, there is no evidence to show that man's intervention was excluded. Secondly, the meaning of Plutarch's text itself is not clear. Delling[213] notes that, in view of what follows ("man"), the notion of "to approach" (a woman) is surprising; furthermore "perhaps in respect to *pneuma* (spirit) we are to think of a divine emanation. At any rate . . . the divine operation is presented in terms which suggest immediacy, though through a very refined matter." Thirdly, the Egyptian belief refers to *pneuma;* oddly enough, Philo does not mention it, though this concept was available to him through the biblical tradition, if not through the Egyptian speculation also. In this respect, Nellessen[214] notes that one can take into consideration that Philo did have the element *pneuma* at his disposal, but he found it disturbing in his system, and therefore he left it out. In his speculation Philo is independent and completely personal. Concern-

---

Jesus 190f: "Nor is it evident that the idea of a virgin birth for Jesus was an import into early Christian thought from the hero legends of the Hellenistic or Near Eastern world. When the parallels that are supposed to have provoked such an idea are closely examined, they turn out to be less than significant for an understanding of the New Testament. Neither Sargon . . . nor the Egyptian pharaohs, nor Buddha . . . nor Augustus, sat for the portrait of mother and child that has been drawn in the infancy narratives of the gospel." Agrees Latke G., 'Lukas 1,' 75ff; Galot J., 'La Conception virginale' 655ff, who notes that recourse to pagan myths to illustrate the virgin birth is as old as Christianity itself.

[213] *ThWNT* V, 528.
[214] Nellessen E., *Das Kind,* 106.

ing the subject of a virgin-birth theologoumenon, "neither is
(Philo) a witness to . . . a tradition of hellenistic Judaism, nor
has he influenced Judaism with his speculations."[215]

As for Gal 4, 29 (Isaac born "according to the Spirit"), it
has been pointed out above that in Paul's view this does by
no means exclude that Abraham was the physical father of
Isaac; besides the fact that his mother's virginity is out of the
question, precisely because she had lived with Abraham long
enough to show that she was unfruitful. That in Gal 4, 29
Paul does not think of a miraculous birth of Isaac can be seen
in the fact that the intention of the context is to show that
Christians are free from the Law, as children and heirs of
Abraham; they are "children of the promise like Isaac" (4,
28), not because of a miraculous birth but because, as they
belong to Christ, they are Abraham's seed. Nor does the idea
of a virginal conception find any support in Gal 4, 27[216] where
Paul, quoting Is 54, 1, refers to the "deserted wife" who has
more children than she who lives with her husband: Is 54, 1 is
quoted here, not because of its reference to the deserted wife,
but because of its reference to the new Jerusalem; the emphasis
falls upon the luck of the previously unfruitful Jerusalem, a
luck which derives from God's promise. On the other hand,
Paul does not elaborate on the "deserted wife," beyond Is. Nor
is there any reason to link Paul—through Is 54, 1—to Philo
when the latter refers to God's visit to Sara "in her solitude"
(*monotheisan;* cfr Gen 21, 1),[217] which is perfectly explained
by the context. Paul, as a result, is no witness to a hellenistic-
Jewish theologoumenon in regard to a conception by the Spirit
(through a virgin).

The final result is that there is no evidence to the effect that
hellenistic Judaism was the vehicle of the Egyptian belief in
a (not necessarily virginal) conception through the Spirit to

---

[215] *Ibid.*
[216] This is the contention of Dibelius M., 'Jungfrauensohn,' 28ff.
[217] *Cher.,* 45.

Christian speculations about Christ's origins. Furthermore, the theme of virginity missing in both Egypt, Philo and Paul, cannot be supplemented by any recourse to an "outdoing" parallelism the purpose of which is to compare John the Baptizer with Christ while emphasizing the excellence of the latter over the former. In fact, the notions of the mother's virginity and of the Spirit's activity are found not only in Lk but also in Mt; now, there is no outdoing parallelism in Mt. On the other hand, the biblical narratives, both in Mt and in Lk, are so steeped in the biblical and Jewish tradition that any recourse to the ideas of virgin births in the mystery religions is beside the point. That the detail of the virgin birth is an exception, should be accurately proved. Moreover, even in the case that such ideas were known to early Christians, this knowledge does not yet prove or imply that they accepted them. In addition, some *elements* common to pagan conceptions and to the Gospel narratives are not enough to contend that we have to deal with the same subject in both cases.

Resorting to theologoumena in order to go around the contents of a given text, is too subjective—and risky—a procedure to be scholarly sound. If theologoumena are to become the methodological *deus ex machina* of exegesis, and of theology in general, all the contents of revelation can be easily volatized by means of this new theological alchemy. There is nothing in the Bible and in revelation that cannot be evaporated into some kind of theologoumenon. Not only Abraham's calling life and promises, not only Isaac's birth and existence—and with them the reality of election and covenant—are gone; not only the mysteries of Christ's life, death and resurrection become a symbol of "nothing" else, but the very existence of Christ can become a theological "allegory" necessary to give some sort of reality to the promises contained in the Old Testament. It is Paul who maintains that "all promises of God are yes in him" in Christ (2 Cor 1, 20), and that Christ is the "one" seed intended by God in all His promises to Abraham

(Gal 3, 16). Why should this not be a theologoumenon or christologoumenon? Obviously, the theologoumenon-methodology marks a gigantic improvement on the Alexandrian allegorizing—but in the same direction away from reality. At this point, Christianity itself becomes another theologoumenon; it volatizes into myth, superstition, nothing.

On the other hand, it is well known that, for the Bible, God expresses His wishes and carries out His design by facts and by real interventions. This is the way God teaches, this is the supreme manner in which God conveys His message to man. The sacred writers were convinced that the ideas they express in their writing are derived from the facts at the basis of their narratives—it is the facts that convey a lesson, it is not the lesson that creates the "facts" (i.e. the symbols or symbolic events which never took place).

The inference is that God's real interest in Christ's birth, and coming in general, is by far more aptly and efficaciously signified by a genuine and factual intervention than through a narrative which has to fabricate an imaginary event where, after all, the message remains highly conceptual and dialectic. Obviously, there is no conflict between the doctrine of God's interest in Christ and God's factual intervention—virginal conception—to make His interest clear. Even more: the only way to signify one's interest in a fully convincing and unequivocal manner is a personal and factual intervention. This is the way God has acted throughout the ages in Salvation History: committing His "power" to His interest.

SCRIPTURE INDEX